PRAY! PRAY! PRAY!

PRAY! PRAY! PRAY!

Compiled by Betsey M. War

Queen of the Apostles Mission Association
8035 S. Quebec
Englewood, CO 80112
Phone (303) 770-3240 FAX (303) 770-0415

Queenship

Publishing Company
P.O. Box 42028
Santa Barbara, Ca. 93140-2028
Phone (800) 647-9882 Fax (805) 569-3274

Cum Permissio

+ Thomas J Curry

Most Reverend Thomas J. Curry
Auxilairy Bishop
Santa Barbara Pastoral Region
Archdiocese of Los Angeles
April 10, 1995

©1995 Queenship Publishing

Library of Congress Catalog Card #: 93-87011

Published by:
Queenship Publishing
P.O. Box 42028
Santa Barbara, CA 93140-2028
Phone: (800) 647-9882 FAX: (805) 569-3274

Printed in the United States of America

ISBN: 1-882972-21-X

ACKNOWLEDGMENTS

The goal of this prayer book is to have available a worship aid for our Thursday Holy Hour and, of course, for private devotions. Originally planned as a limited devotional aid it has grown to its present size.

These pages contain prayers, meditations, litanies and hymns drawn from a wide range of sources, popular in Catholic worship throughout the years.

It is hoped this prayer book will help to promote Eucharistic and Marian devotions as our Blessed Mother calls us to her Son, present in the Eucharist. It is my hope that it will bring all of us to the Sacred Heart of Jesus and the Immaculate Heart of Mary.

This labor of love would have been impossible without the love and guidance of Our Lord Jesus, His mother Mary and the inspiration of the Holy Spirit.

This prayer book could not have been compiled without the help of Colleen Graybeal, who did all the typing and Lillian Balint and Billie Helfert who did the proof-reading. I thank them for their love, support and cooperation.

v

I also wish to thank those who prayed and gave us encouragement for the success of this prayer book.

I further acknowledge the gifts of all the contributors for their cooperation and permission for their works to be used in this prayer book.

Betsey M. War

DEDICATION

PRAY! PRAY! PRAY!
PRAYER BOOK

We dedicate this prayer book to Our Holy Father, Pope John Paul II, with all our love to help in the conversion and evangelization of Russia which was asked for at Fatima in 1917 by Our Blessed Mother. Through this conversion will come the Triumph of Her Immaculate Heart and that, in turn, will usher in the reign of the Sacred Heart of Jesus.

Pope John Paul II is teaching us by example how to live totally consecrated to Jesus through Mary. We pray that under his pontificate the triumph will come.

Praised be Jesus and Mary.

vii

"TO OUR LADY"

Lovely Lady dressed in blue,
Teach me how to pray!
God was just your little Boy,
Tell me what to say!

Did you lift Him up sometimes,
Gently, on your knee?
Did you sing to Him the way
Mother does to me?

Did you hold His hand at night?
Did you ever try
Telling stories of the world?
O! And did He cry?

Do you really think He cares
I tell Him things—
Little things that happen?
And do the Angels' wings

Make a noise? And can He hear
Me if I speak low?
Does He understand me now?
Tell me— for you know?

Lovely Lady dressed in blue,
Teach me how to pray!
God was just your little Boy.
And you know the way.

viii

ROSEBUD PRAYER

It's only a tiny rosebud,
a flower of God's design;
but I can't unfold the petals,
with these clumsy hands of mine.

The secret of unfolding flowers
is not known to such as I,
the flowers God opens so sweetly;
in my hands would fade and die.

If I can't unfold a rosebud
this flower of God's design
then how can I think I have the wisdom
to unfold this life of mine?

So I'll trust in Him for His leading
each moment of every day,
and I'll look to Him for His wisdom
each step of the pilgrim way.

For the pathway that lies before me
my Heavenly Father knows,
I will trust Him to unfold the moments
first as He unfolds the rose.

Author Unknown

A PRAYER FOR TODAY

This is the beginning of a new day.
God has given us this day to use as we will.
We can waste it ~ or use it for good,
but what we do today is important
because we are exchanging a day of our
life for it! When tomorrow comes,
this day will be gone forever, leaving in
its place something that we have traded
for it. We want it to be gain, and not loss;
good and not evil; success and not failure;
in order that we shall not regret the price
we have paid for it.

Author Unknown

x

TABLE OF CONTENTS

INDEX TO PRAYERS

xiii

OUR LADY OF FATIMA

MESSAGES OF OUR
LADY OF FATIMA

In these times, Our Lady comes to remind us of Her Fatima message and to encourage all Her children to comply with Her request wholeheartedly.

We invite you, we implore you, to join with us in our prayer so that Our Lady's promise of a time of peace will come...in our lifetime, for our children.

MAY 13, 1917 - OCTOBER 13, 1917

"Tell everybody that God gives graces through the Immaculate Heart of Mary. Tell them to ask graces from her, and that the Heart of Jesus wishes to be venerated together with the Immaculate Heart of Mary, for the Lord has confided the peace of the world to her."

"I promise to help at the hour of death, with graces needed for salvation, whoever, on the FIRST SATURDAY of 5 consecutive months, shall confess and receive Holy Communion, recite 5 decades of the Rosary, and keep me company for 15 minutes, while meditating on the mysteries of the Rosary with the intention of making reparation to My Immaculate Heart."

"If my requests are not granted, Russia will scatter her errors throughout the world, provoking wars and persecutions of the Church. The good will be martyred, the Holy Father will have much to suffer, and various nations will be destroyed!"

"In the end My Immaculate Heart will triumph, the Holy Father will consecrate Russia to me, Russia will be converted, and a certain period of peace will be granted to the world!"

"I am the Lady of the Rosary, I have come to warn the faithful to amend their lives and to ask pardon for their sins. They must not offend Our Lord any more, for He is already too grievously offended by the sins of men. People must say the Rosary. Let them continue saying it every day."

≈≈≈≈≈≈≈≈≈≈≈≈≈≈≈≈≈≈≈≈≈≈≈≈≈≈≈≈≈≈≈≈≈≈≈≈≈≈≈

"Jesus, Mary and Joseph, I love you, save souls."
(Fatima request)

Jesus, Savior of the World, Save Russia.

TOTAL CONSECRATION TO JESUS
THROUGH MARY

Pope John Paul II gives Our Lady credit for his ministry and the ability he has had to respond to the message of the Gospel with strength and courage. Pope John Paul II has made the Total Consecration, according to the formula recommended by St. Louis DeMontfort as a young man and he felt profound changes in the direction taken by his life.

Our Holy Father has as part of his crest "TOTUS TUUS," "TOTALLY YOURS," referring to his consecration to Our Lady.

The TOTAL CONSECRATION is the deepest commitment, the deepest gift we can give to God the Father. By consecrating ourselves to His Son, Our Lord Jesus Christ, through Mary, the Immaculate Conception, we honor all that He has given us and glorify Him with the gift of our lives and our hearts.

Please join in this global effort to bring all her children under her mantle so that she can use us more perfectly in the battle between good and evil, in the march toward the TRIUMPH OF HER IMMACULATE HEART AND THE REIGN OF THE SACRED HEART OF JESUS!

Our Lady has blessed and challenged us to work diligently and prayerfully for her Triumph. She told us in Fatima that it will come when the Holy Father consecrates Russia to her Immaculate Heart and Russia is converted. Our promise from her is peace, GLOBAL PEACE! The challenge is awesome and yet we feel confident that, as promised at Fatima, her Immaculate Heart will triumph and we offer ourselves as her instruments in helping to bring it about. We ask you all to join us in this mission.

We will form the remnant church and will be known by the 3 marks:

1. Great reverence for the true presence of Jesus in the Holy Eucharist.
2. Fidelity to the Holy Father, the Vicar of Christ.
3. Devotion to the Immaculate Heart of Mary.

XX

AGENDA FOR HOLY HOUR

Opening Song

The Most Holy Rosary of the Blessed
   Virgin Mary and Meditations.
    Responses (Blessed Sacrament Prayers)

Celebrant Enters (incensing and song optional)
    (O Saving Victim)
    or other suitable Eucharistic selection

Litanies (Choose A, B, C, D, E or F)

Scripture, Homily, or Quiet Time

1

COMMUNITY HOLY HOUR

Now let us lift our hearts and souls in prayer, praying especially for:

THE CONVERSION OF RUSSIA.
THE TRIUMPH OF THE IMMACULATE
HEART OF MARY.
THE REIGN OF THE SACRED HEART OF
JESUS.

OPENING PRAYER:

Father, we thank You for the gift of Your Son in the Most Holy Eucharist. Spirit of Jesus, we ask that you fill us with blessings and gifts founded in love in the Most Holy Trinity.

We pray for all of our brothers and sisters, here in the parish and throughout the world, that our hearts may turn to you; that our souls may be sanctified; that we may become the perfect image of You, Most Heavenly Father.

You have called us to be Your sons and daughters, united in the Spirit. Our brothers and sisters in Russia have suffered persecution for 75 years because You have been denied. In Your great mercy, though, You have allowed Mary, the Mother of Your Son, and our Mother, to come to earth and call us to pray for the conversion of Russia.

With all our hearts, we unite our voices in prayer and raise them to you. Send Your Holy Spirit upon the people of Russia. Feed them with Your Body; give them Your Blood as drink. Heal them, Lord God, and restore them. We ask this through Our Lord and Savior, Jesus Christ. Amen.

≈≈≈≈≈≈≈≈≈≈≈≈≈≈≈≈≈≈≈≈≈≈≈≈≈≈≈≈≈≈≈≈≈≈≈≈≈≈≈

The Most Holy Rosary of The Blessed Virgin Mary and Meditations

≈≈≈≈≈≈≈≈≈≈≈≈≈≈≈≈≈≈≈≈≈≈≈≈≈≈≈≈≈≈≈≈≈≈≈≈≈≈≈

(AFTER EACH DECADE SAY): "O my Jesus, forgive us our sins, save us from the fires of hell, lead all souls to heaven, especially those in most need of your mercy.

THE LECTOR MAY READ A MEDITATION RELATING EACH MYSTERY WITH OUR PRESENCE BEFORE THE BLESSED SACRAMENT. FOLLOWING EACH MEDITATION, ALL PRAY THE BLESSED SACRAMENT PRAYER TOGETHER, AND THEN RECITE A DECADE OF THE ROSARY.

SCRIPTURAL MEDITATIONS ON THE JOYFUL MYSTERIES

(The Lector may read a meditation before each decade of the Rosary)

I. THE ANNUNCIATION
(HUMILITY)
(Listen to a meditation)

BLESSED SACRAMENT PRAYER**

ALL: Aware of Your loving Presence, Jesus, we unite ourselves to the obedience of Mary and offer You her perfect "Yes" to repair for our lack of responding wholeheartedly to Your will in all things. "TEACH ME TO DO YOUR WILL, FOR YOU, O LORD ARE MY GOD." May we become docile and prompt in doing Your holy will always. MAKE ME KNOW THE WAY I SHOULD WALK; TO YOU, I LIFT UP MY SOUL." "YOUR WILL IS MY HERITAGE FOREVER, THE JOY OF MY HEART." With each "Hail Mary" of this mystery, we say "Yes" to all you want us to be and do.

(Now recite the first decade of the Rosary)

**Used with written permission of Reverend Martin Lucia SS.CC. of the Apostolate of Perpetual Adoration.

5

II . THE VISITATION OF MARY
(FRATERNAL CHARITY)
(Listen to a meditation)

BLESSED SACRAMENT PRAYER **

ALL: Jesus, we unite ourselves to the perfect trust of Mary and pray through her intercession that our trust may become perfect too. "I TRUST IN THE GOODNESS OF GOD FOR EVER AND EVER." By the infinite power of Your Eucharistic love, we beg you, Jesus, to capture, conquer, and cast out every doubt, fear, and anxiety that we have so that Your peace may reign in our hearts. "CAST ALL YOUR ANXIETY UPON THE LORD, WHO CARES FOR YOU."

(Now recite the second decade of the Rosary)

** Used with permission

III. THE BIRTH OF JESUS
(LOVE OF GOD)
(Listen to a meditation)

BLESSED SACRAMENT PRAYER**

ALL: Jesus, with each "Hail Mary" we pray, we unite ourselves to the perfect adoration of Mary, and offer You all the adoration she gave to You in Bethlehem that we may bring to you now all the joy and warmth that her adoration brought to you on that first Christmas night when she held you in her arms and brought You close to her heart. We thank You and praise You with all the affection of Mary for being born in Bethlehem and becoming one like us, and for continuing Your incarnation among us here in this Blessed Sacrament. Teach us to value and cherish Your Eucharistic Presence so that Your Eucharistic love influences our every thought, word, and deed until our whole life becomes adoration "IN SPIRIT AND IN TRUTH."

(Now recite the third decade of the Rosary)

** Used with permission

7

IV. THE PRESENTATION AND CONSECRATION OF JESUS IN THE TEMPLE (OBEDIENCE)

(Listen to a meditation)

BLESSED SACRAMENT PRAYER**

ALL: Jesus, take our wretched hearts, and give us a "new heart" by giving us Your very own. During this mystery, we renew our total consecration to the Immaculate Heart of Mary. Through Mary, we offer to Your Eucharistic Heart, all that we have, and all that we are, "totally Yours, totus tuus."

(Now recite the fourth decade of the Rosary)

** Used with permission

8

V. THE FINDING OF JESUS
IN THE TEMPLE
(JOY)
(Listen to a meditation)

BLESSED SACRAMENT PRAYER**

ALL: Jesus, through the Heart of Mary, we beg you to lead all men to Yourself in this most Blessed Sacrament, for you will "THAT ALL MEN BE SAVED AND COME TO THE KNOWLEDGE OF THE TRUTH." We lift up to Your Eucharistic Heart all those who have experienced a loss of any kind and beg you to restore all that has been lost, for you promised: "IF MY PEOPLE, WHO BEAR MY NAME, HUMBLE THEMSELVES, AND PRAY AND SEEK MY PRESENCE, AND TURN FROM THEIR WICKED WAYS, I MYSELF WILL HEAR FROM HEAVEN AND FORGIVE THEIR SINS AND RESTORE THEIR LAND."

(Now recite the fifth decade of the Rosary)

** Used with permission

9

PRAYER TO THE SACRED HEART

Oh Sacred Heart of Jesus I've placed my trust in Thee.

Whatever may befall me Lord, tho dark the hour may be in all my cares, in all my woes, tho naught but grief I see Oh Sacred Heart of Jesus I've placed my trust in Thee.

When those I love have passed away and I am sore distressed, Oh Sacred Heart of Jesus I fly to Thee for rest.

In all my trials, great or small, my confidence shall be unshaken as I cry dear Lord - I've placed my trust in Thee.

This is my own sween prayer dear lord, my faith my trust, my love.

And most of all in that last hour when Death points up above Oh then sweet Savior may thy face smile on my soul set free.

And may I cry with rapturous love Oh Sacred Heart of Jesus I've placed my trust in Thee!

SCRIPTURAL MEDITATIONS ON THE SORROWFUL MYSTERIES

*(The Lector may read a meditation
before each decade of the Rosary)*

I. THE AGONY IN THE GARDEN (TRUE REPENTANCE)
(Listen to a meditation)

BLESSED SACRAMENT PRAYER**

ALL: Conscious of Your loving Presence, Jesus, we unite ourselves deeply to Your attitude in the garden when You prayed: "FATHER, NOT MY WILL, BUT YOUR WILL BE DONE." During this decade, we offer You the perfect love of Mary to make up for what is lacking in our own hearts and to repair for all of the rejection that You receive from the world in this Sacrament of Your love. With each "Hail Mary" of this mystery, we pray in our heart: may the Heart of Jesus in the most Blessed Sacrament be praised adored and loved with grateful affection at every moment in all the tabernacles of the world, even to the end of time.

(Now recite the first decade of the Rosary)

**Used with permission

II . THE SCOURGING AT THE PILLAR
(PURITY)
(Listen to a meditation)

BLESSED SACRAMENT PRAYER**

ALL: Jesus, by the physical wounds You suffered at
the pillar, help us to overcome the inclinations of
the flesh that we may live in Your Spirit and prefer
Your Love to all other loves. Through Mary, we
pray that we may be pure in thought and deed.
Through Mary, we pray for a deep understanding of
Your personal love for us in the Holy Eucharist;
that, like her, we may respond to You with our
whole heart.

Cleanse us of all false idols so that Your love
and Presence in the Eucharist may animate us and
become the treasure of our heart. "A PURE HEART
CREATE FOR ME, O GOD; A STEADFAST
SPIRIT RENEW IN ME."

(Now recite the second decade of the Rosary)

**Used with permission

12

III. THE CROWNING WITH THORNS
(MORAL COURAGE)
(Listen to a meditation)

BLESSED SACRAMENT PRAYER**

ALL: Jesus, awakened to Your great love for us, we offer You the perfect gratitude of Mary in reparation for the indifference and ingratitude of the world toward your love in the Holy Eucharist. By Your crown of thorns, make us humble, Jesus, that we may imitate Your humility in the Eucharist. We thank You with the Heart of Mary on each bead of this mystery for all You have done for our salvation, and for the gift of Yourself in this most Blessed Sacrament.

(Recite the third decade of the Rosary)

**Used with permission

13

IV. JESUS CARRIES THE CROSS
(PATIENCE)
(Listen to a meditation)

BLESSED SACRAMENT PRAYER**

ALL: Jesus, during this mystery, we embrace our cross for love of You, Who kissed and embraced Your Cross for love of us. With Your grace, help us to fulfill our daily duties in life. We renew our baptismal vows and ask You to prepare our hearts for a worthy confession where You wash away our sins in Your Blood. With the strength of this most Blessed Sacrament, we beg You for the courage to TAKE UP OUR CROSS EACH DAY AND FOLLOW YOU that we may be Your disciples. We are weak, but You are strong! By Your falling three times and getting up again, we beg you through the motherly Heart of Mary to pour out from Your Eucharistic Heart the abundance of strength and consolation upon all of the depressed and discouraged in the world, especially those who have fallen into despair and who are in most need of Your encouragement.

(Now recite the fourth decade of the Rosary)

**Used with permission

V. THE CRUCIFIXION AND DEATH OF JESUS ON THE CROSS. (FINAL PERSEVERANCE)

(Listen to a meditation)

BLESSED SACRAMENT PRAYER**

ALL: On each bead of this mystery, Jesus, we offer You all the comfort of Your Holy Mother, who stood by You when You were alone and abandoned on the Cross, for again You are alone and abandoned in so many tabernacles of the world. O Jesus, look at the tears of Your Holy Mother. In union with the infinite value of each Mass until the end of time, we beg You to DRAW ALL MEN TO YOUR EUCHARISTIC HEART for you have said: "WHEN I AM LIFTED UP FROM THE EARTH, I WILL DRAW ALL MEN TO MYSELF."

(Now recite the fifth decade of the Rosary)

**Used with permission

15

Joan Camerom Mitchell

16

SCRIPTURAL MEDITATIONS ON THE GLORIOUS MYSTERIES

(The Lector may read a mediation before each decade of the Rosary)

I. THE RESURRECTION (FAITH)
(Listen to a meditation)

BLESSED SACRAMENT PRAYER**

ALL: Jesus, increase our faith in Your Real Presence in the Blessed Sacrament, the mystery of faith, that like the disciples who came to know You "in the breaking of the Bread", we may come to know You in the Eucharist in an intimate and personal way with a deep and living faith that grows to conviction about the things we do not see and enables us to experience the sweetness of Your love "which surpasses all knowledge." We pray through the Immaculate Heart of Mary that You help our parish and all parishes to become a faith community by responding to Your appeal to be loved day and night in this most Blessed Sacrament, where You call us to "pray without ceasing." This is where You, Our Risen Savior, dwell helping us by the power of Your sufferings, that we may share also in the glory of Your resurrection. On each bead of this mystery, deepen our union with You until our single-hearted prayer becomes "ALL I WANT IS TO KNOW CHRIST JESUS...."

(Now recite the first decade of the Rosary)

**Used with permission

II. THE ASCENSION
(HOPE)
(Listen to a meditation)

BLESSED SACRAMENT PRAYER**

ALL: Jesus, increase our hope and center it in Your Eucharistic love. We beg You, through Mary, to bring hope to all mankind. During this mystery, we offer You the many hours Mary spent in Your Eucharistic presence during her life on earth, that we may give to You now, in our Holy Hour of Prayer, all the glory that she gave to you then! We unite ourselves to the perfect appreciation of Mary who found her rest, her peace, her joy, and her fulfillment in Your Eucharistic Presence, our heaven on earth.

(Now recite the second decade of the Rosary)

**Used with permission

18

III. THE DESCENT OF THE HOLY SPIRIT UPON MARY AND THE APOSTLES (ZEAL)

(Listen to a meditation)

BLESSED SACRAMENT PRAYER**

ALL: Eucharistic Heart of Jesus, divine furnace of charity, inflame my heart with perfect love for You. I give You all that is unclean and ugly within me in exchange for all that is pure and beautiful within You. Jesus, make me holy, and make my heart so like unto Yours that Your love will shine through me, like a light through a window, so that others may see You in me. Like a monstrance, may I show You to the world. Through Mary, the spouse of the Holy Spirit, we pray for a new Pentecost today where You send Your Spirit to everyone. May the fire of Your Divine love, like the rays of the sun which shine on all, go out to touch, bless, help and heal everyone. May the Holy Spirit, which flows from Your Eucharistic Heart COME TO EACH ONE AND RENEW THE FACE OF THE EARTH that there may be but "one flock and one Shepherd."

(Now recite the third decade of the Rosary)

**Used with permission

IV. THE ASSUMPTION OF THE BLESSED VIRGIN MARY INTO HEAVEN (GRACE OF A HAPPY DEATH)

(Listen to a meditation)

BLESSED SACRAMENT PRAYER**

ALL: Jesus, on each "Hail Mary" of this mystery, we offer to You the love of Mary to make up for what is lacking in our own hearts that we may love You now in the Blessed Sacrament with the perfect love of Her Immaculate Heart. This begins our heaven on earth: loving You, Jesus, with the Heart of Mary. Through Mary, I can say: Jesus, with all my heart I love You as I now make a spiritual communion with You. "ANYONE WHO LOVES ME WILL BE TRUE TO MY WORD, AND MY FATHER WILL LOVE HIM; WE WILL COME TO HIM AND MAKE OUR DWELLING PLACE WITH HIM." With each "Hail Mary", deepen my personal relationship with you. May a constant communion with You on earth be a foretaste of my union with You in Heaven. Jesus, we pray by the infinite merits of Your Sacred Heart and the merits of the Immaculate Heart of Mary that all may be made ONE with You in this most Holy Eucharist.

(Now recite the fourth decade of the Rosary)

**Used with permission

V. THE CORONATION OF THE BLESSED VIRGIN, QUEEN OF HEAVEN AND EARTH (TRUST AND LOVE FOR MARY)
(Listen to a meditation)

BLESSED SACRAMENT PRAYER**

ALL: Jesus, through Mary, we humbly surrender our hearts to You, that we may live the gospel, the whole gospel, in the whole of our life, in response to the Eucharist where You give Your Heart to us. This sacrament contains all that You have and all that You are, the entire spiritual wealth of the Church. "GOOD MEASURE, PRESSED DOWN, AND RUNNING OVER." Jesus, during this mystery, we pray with confidence FOR THE TRIUMPH OF THE IMMACULATE HEART OF MARY, AND THE REIGN OF YOUR MOST SACRED HEART, in every heart "that God may be all in all."

(Now recite the fifth decade of the Rosary)

**Used with permission

21

HAIL HOLY QUEEN

Hail, Holy Queen, Mother of Mercy; our life, our sweetness, and our hope! To you do we cry, poor banished children of Eve. To you do we send up our sighs, mourning and weeping in this vale of tears. Turn then, most gracious advocate, your eyes of mercy towards us; and after this our exile, show to us the blessed fruit of your womb, Jesus. O clement, O loving, O sweet Virgin Mary.

V. Pray for us, O holy Mother of God.
R. That we may be made worthy of the promises of Christ.

PRAYER AFTER THE ROSARY

O God, whose only-begotten Son, by His life, death and resurrection, has purchased for us the rewards of eternal life; grant, we beseech Thee, that, meditating upon these mysteries of the Most Holy Rosary of the Blessed Virgin Mary, we may imitate what they contain and obtain what they promise, through the same Christ our Lord. Amen.

Prayers for the Holy Father
Our Father
Hail Mary
Glory Be

(CHOOSE A, B, C, OR D)

("A")

LITANY OF THE SACRED HEART

Lord, have mercy on us.
Christ, have mercy on us.
Lord, have mercy on us. Christ hear us.
Christ, graciously hear us.

R. *HAVE MERCY ON US.*

God, the Father of Heaven.....
God, the Son, Redeemer of the world.....
God, the Holy Spirit.....
Holy Trinity, one God.....
Heart of Jesus, Son of the Eternal Father.....
Heart of Jesus, formed by the Holy Spirit, in the
    womb of the Virgin Mother.....
Heart of Jesus, substantially united to the Word
    of God.....
Heart of Jesus, of Infinite Majesty.....
Heart of Jesus, Holy Temple of God.....
Heart of Jesus, Tabernacle of the Most High.....
Heart of Jesus, House of God and Gate
    of Heaven.....
Heart of Jesus, burning furnace of Charity.....

23

Heart of Jesus, abode of Justice and Love..

Heart of Jesus, full of Goodness and Love.....

Heart of Jesus, abyss of all virtues.....

Heart of Jesus, most worthy of all praise.....

Heart of Jesus, King and center of all hearts.....

Heart of Jesus, in whom are all the treasures
of wisdom and knowledge.....

Heart of Jesus, in whom dwells the fullness
of Divinity.....

Heart of Jesus, in Whom the Father was
well pleased.....

Heart of Jesus, of Whose fullness we have
all received.....

Heart of Jesus, desire of the everlasting hills.....

Heart of Jesus, patient and full of Mercy.....

Heart of Jesus, enriching all who invoke you.....

Heart of Jesus, fountain of life and holiness.....

Heart of Jesus, propitiation for our sins.....

Heart of Jesus, loaded down with reproaches.....

Heart of Jesus, bruised for our offenses.....

Heart of Jesus, obedient unto death.....

Heart of Jesus, pierced with a lance.....

Heart of Jesus, source of all consolation.....

Heart of Jesus, our life and resurrection.....

Heart of Jesus, our peace and reconciliation.....

Heart of Jesus, victim of sin.....

Heart of Jesus, salvation of those who trust in You.....

Heart of Jesus, hope of those who die in You.....
Heart of Jesus, delight of all the saints.....

Lamb of God, who takes away the sins of the world.
Spare us, O Lord.
Lamb of God, who takes away the sins of the world.
Graciously hear us, O Lord,
Lamb of God, who takes away the sins of the world.
Have mercy on us.

Priest or Deacon Recites

Let us pray; O Almighty and Eternal God, look
upon the heart of Your dearly beloved Son and upon
the praise and satisfaction He offers You in the
name of sinners and for those who seek Your mercy.
Be appeased and grant us pardon in the name of the
same Jesus Christ, Your Son, Who Lives and reigns
with You, in the Unity of the Holy Spirit, one God,
world without end. Amen.

Statue of the Sacred Heart of Jesus at Mother
Cabrini Shrine in Golden, Colorado

LITANY OF THE SACRED HEART
by
ST. FRANCES XAVIER CABRINI**

Lovable Heart of Jesus, attract me;
All-powerful Heart of Jesus, win me to Yourself;
Unchanging Heart of Jesus, keep me constant;
Immensity of the Heart of Jesus, fill me;
Holiness of the Heart of Jesus, make me holy;
Providence of the Heart of Jesus, assist me;
Obedience of the Heart of Jesus, make me docile;
Silence of the Heart of Jesus, teach me;
Sweetness of the Heart of Jesus, make me gentle;
Purity of the Heart of Jesus, purify me;
Patience of the Heart of Jesus, bear with me;
Desires of the heart of Jesus, rule in me;
Flames of the Heart of Jesus, ignite me;
Kindness of the Heart of Jesus, encircle me;
Sufferings of the Heart of Jesus, make me
      compassionate;
Riches of the Heart of Jesus, satisfy me;
Humiliations of the Heart of Jesus, overwhelm me;
Graces of the Heart of Jesus, flood me;
Sacred Heart of my King, possess me;

**Used with permission

Sacred Heart of my Father, give me life;
Sacred Heart of my Teacher, instruct me;
Sacred Heart of my Guide, lead me;
Sacred Heart of my physician, heal me
Sacred Heart of my Judge, pardon me;
Sacred Heart of my Savior, save me;
Sacred Heart of my God, be my All;
Sacred Heart of my All, Make me Yours.

Roses used with permission of Debbie War Scott

("C")

LITANY OF SAINT JOSEPH

Saint Joseph died in the arms of Jesus and Mary. He is, therefore, the patron of a happy death. Pray to him to obtain for you this favor.

Lord, have mercy on us.
Christ, have mercy on us.
Lord, have mercy on us.
Christ, hear us.
Christ, graciously hear us.
God the Father of Heaven, *have mercy on us.*
God the Son, Redeemer of the world,
      have mercy on us.
God the Holy Ghost, *have mercy on us.*
Holy Trinity, one God, *have mercy on us.*
Holy Mary, *pray for us.*
R. PRAY FOR US
Holy Joseph.....
Noble scion of David.....
Light of the Patriarchs.....
Spouse of the Mother of God.....
Chaste Guardian of the Virgin.....
Foster -Father of the Son of God, Head of the
      Holy Family.....
Joseph most just.....

29

Diligent Defender of Christ.....
Joseph most chaste.....
Joseph most prudent.....
Joseph most valiant.....
Joseph most obedient.....
Joseph most faithful.....
Mirror of Patience.....
Lover of Poverty.....
Model of laborers.....
Ornament of domestic life.....
Protector of virgins.....
Pillar of families.....
Consolation of the afflicted.....
Hope of the sick.....
Patron of the dying.....
Terror of the demons.....
Protector of the Holy Church.....
Lamb of God, who takes away the sins of the world, *spare us, O Lord.*
Lamb of God, who takes away the sins of the world, *graciously hear us O Lord.*
Lamb of God, who takes away the sins of the world, *have mercy on us, O Lord.*

V. He had made him master of His house.
P. And ruler of all his possessions.

Let us pray

O God, who didst deign to elect Blessed Joseph spouse of Thy most holy Mother, grant, we beseech Thee, that we may have him, whom we venerate as our protector on earth, as our intercessor in heaven. Who livest and reignest world without end. Amen.

≈≈≈≈≈≈≈≈≈≈≈≈≈≈≈≈≈≈≈≈≈≈≈≈≈≈≈≈≈≈≈≈≈≈≈≈≈

St. Joseph, is still with us today as a perfect reflection of the Fatherhood of God, and as a model of Fatherhood for all mankind. He resembles Jesus Himself, who is the perfect image of God the Father and the spiritual Father of all of us.

INVOCATION TO ST. JOSEPH

Obtain for us, dear Joseph, grace to lead an innocent life; and may we ever be shielded by your patronage.

"St. Joseph, head of the Holy Family, Pray for us."

("D")

LITANY OF THE PRECIOUS BLOOD OF JESUS

Lord, have mercy.
Christ, have mercy.
Lord, have mercy. Christ hear us.
Christ, graciously hear us.
God the Father of Heaven, *have mercy on us.*
God the Son, Redeemer of the world, *have mercy on us.*
God, the Holy Spirit, *have mercy on us.*
Holy Trinity, One God, *have mercy on us.*
Blood of Christ, Only-Begotten Son of the Eternal
    Father, *save us.*
Blood of Christ, Incarnate Word of God, *save us.*
Blood of Christ, of the New and Eternal Testament,
    save us.
Blood of Christ, falling upon the earth in the Agony,
    save us.
Blood of Christ, shed profusely in the Scourging,
    save us.
Blood of Christ, flowing forth in the Crowning with
    Thorns, *Save us.*
Blood of Christ, poured out on the Cross, *save us.*
Blood of Christ, Price of our Salvation, *save us.*
Blood of Christ, without which there is no
    forgiveness, *save us.*

Blood of Christ, Eucharistic drink and refreshment
of souls, *save us.*
Blood of Christ, river of Mercy, *save us.*
Blood of Christ, Victor over demons, *save us.*
Blood of Christ, Courage of Martyrs, *save us.*
Blood of Christ, Strength of Confessors, *save us.*
Blood of Christ, bringing forth Virgins, *save us.*
Blood of Christ, Help of those in peril, *save us.*
Blood of Christ, Relief of the burdened, *save us.*
Blood of Christ, Solace in sorrow, *save us.*
Blood of Christ, Hope of the penitent, *save us.*
Blood of Christ, Consolation of the dying, *save us.*
Blood of Christ, Peace and Tenderness of hearts,
save us.
Blood of Christ, Pledge of Eternal Life, *save us.*
Blood of Christ, freeing souls from Purgatory,
save us.
Blood of Christ, most worthy of all glory and honor,
save us.
Lamb of God, Who takest away the sins of the
world, *spare us, O Lord.*
Lamb of God, Who takest away the sins of the
world, *graciously hear us, O Lord.*
Lamb of God, Who takest away the sins of the
world, *have Mercy on us.*

Thou hast redeemed us, O Lord, in Thy Blood,
And made of us a kingdom for our God.

Let us pray.

Almighty and Eternal God, Thou hast appointed
Thine Only-Begotten Son the Redeemer of the
world, and willed to be appeased by His Blood.
Grant, we beseech Thee, that we may worthily
adore this Price of our Salvation, and through Its
Power be safeguarded from the evils of this present
life, so that we may rejoice in Its Fruits forever in
Heaven. Through the same Christ Our Lord. *Amen.*

SCRIPTURE, HOMILY OR QUIET TIME
(The priest or deacon may choose to read scripture,
give a teaching, or allow reflection time.)

LITANY OF THE BLESSED VIRGIN MARY

Lord, have mercy on us.
Christ, have mercy on us.
Lord, have mercy on us.
Christ, hear us.
Christ, graciously hear us.
God the Father of Heaven,
Have mercy on us.
God the Son, Redeemer of the world,
have mercy on us.
God the Holy Ghost,
have mercy on us.
Holy Trinity, one God,
have mercy on us.
Holy Mary, *pray for us.*
Holy Mother of God, *pray for us.*
Holy Virgin of virgins, *etc.*
Mother of Christ,
Mother of divine grace,
Mother most pure,
Mother most chaste,
Mother inviolate,
Mother undefiled,
Mother most amiable,
Mother most admirable,
Mother of good counsel,

Mother of our Creator, *pray for us.*
Mother of our Savior, *etc.*
Virgin most prudent,
Virgin most venerable,
Virgin most renowned,
Virgin most powerful,
Virgin most merciful,
Virgin most faithful,
Mirror of justice,
Seat of wisdom,
Cause of our joy,
Spiritual vessel,
Vessel of honor,
Singular vessel of devotion,
Mystical rose,
Towe of David
Tower of ivory,
House of gold,
Ark of the Covenant,
Gate of Heaven,
Morning Star,
Health of the sick,
Refuge of sinners,
Comforter of the afflicted,
Help of Christians,
Queen of angels,
Queen of patriarchs,
Queen of prophets,
Queen of apostles,
Queen of martyrs,

Queen of confessors, *pray for us.*
Queen of virgins, *etc.*
Queen of all saints,
Queen conceived without
    Original Sin,
Queen assumed into Heaven,
Queen of the most holy Rosary,
Queen of peace,
Lamb of God, who takest away
the sins of the world,
    spare us, O Lord.
Lamb of God, who takest away
the sins of the world,
    graciously hear us, O Lord.
Lamb of God, who takest away
    the sins of the world,
    have mercy on us.
Christ graciously hear us.
Pray for us, O Holy Mother of God,
    *That we may be made worthy of
    the promises of Christ.*
Let us pray.
Grant we beseech Thee, O Lord God,
that we Thy servants may enjoy perpetual health of
mind and body and by the glorious intercession of
the Blessed Mary, ever Virgin, be delivered from
present sorrow and enjoy eternal happiness.
Through Christ Our Lord. Amen.

PRAYERS
(Optional Each Week -A, B, C, or D)

("A")

A SPIRITUAL COMMUNION

My Jesus, I believe that you are present in the Most Holy Sacrament. I love You above all things, and I desire to receive You into my soul. Since I cannot at this moment receive You sacramentally, come at least spiritually into my heart. I embrace You as if You were already there and unite myself wholly to You; never permit me to be separated from You.

("A")

I believe that You, O Jesus, are in the most holy Sacrament. I love You and desire You. Come into my heart. I embrace You. Oh, never leave me. May the burning and most sweet power of Your love, O Lord Jesus Christ, I beseech You, absorb my mind that I may always respond to your love for me. Lord Jesus, I love You!

— St. Francis

("B")

AN OFFERING OF SELF

Take, O Lord, into your hands my entire liberty, my memory, my understanding, my will. All that I am and have, You have given me, and I surrender them to You, to be so disposed in accordance with Your Holy Will.

("B")

ACT OF ADORATION

Jesus, My God, I adore You here present in the Blessed Sacrament of the Altar, where You wait day and night to be our comfort, while we await Your unveiled presence in heaven.

Jesus, my God, I adore You in all places where the Blessed Sacrament is reserved and where sins are committed against this sacrament of love.

Jesus, My God, I adore You for all time, past, present, and future, for every soul that ever was, is or shall be created.

Jesus, My God, who for my sake has deigned to subject Yourself to the humiliation of temptation, to the perfidy and defection of friends, to the scorn of Your enemies, I adore You.

Jesus, my God, who for us has endured the buffeting of Your weight of the cross, I adore You.

Jesus, my God, Who for my salvation and that of all mankind, was cruelly nailed to the cross and hung there for three long hours in bitter agony, I adore You.

Jesus, my God, who for love of us did institute this Blessed Sacrament and offer Yourself daily for the sins of men. I adore You.

Jesus, my God, Who in Holy Communion became the food of my soul, I adore You.

Jesus, for You I live, Jesus, for You I die. Jesus, I am yours in life and in death.

PRAYER OF POPE JOHN PAUL II
FOR THE FAMILY

Lord God, from You every family in heaven and on earth takes its name. Father, You are love and life.

Through Your Son, Jesus Christ, born of woman, and through the Holy Spirit, the fountain of divine charity, grant that every family on earth may become for each successive generation a true shrine of life and love.

Grant that Your grace may guide the thoughts and actions of husbands and wives for the good of their families and of all the families in the world.

Grant that the young may find in the family solid support for their human dignity and for their growth in truth and love.

Grant that love, strengthened by the grace of the sacrament of marriage, may prove mightier than all the weaknesses and trials through which our families sometimes pass.

Through the intercession of the Holy Family of Nazareth, grant that the Church may fruitfully carry out her worldwide mission in the family and through the family

We ask this of You, who is life, truth, and love with the Son and the Holy Spirit. Amen.

*Pope John Paul II and his priests at the
Consecration of the Mass.*

HOLY COMMUNION IN UNION WITH THE IMMACULATE HEART OF MARY

To Jesus:

Jesus, how utterly helpless I am to prepare a worthy dwelling for You in my soul. I cannot offer You the faith and humility, the love and ardent desires which You have a right to expect from me.

I renounce myself and all that is evil in me, and I am heartily sorry that I have ever offended You, my highest Good. I take refuge in her whom You have always loved - Mary, Your Mother, whom you have given me as my Mother also. In union with her, I will receive You into my heart.

Jesus, Eternal Wisdom, splendor of the Father, You are the Word of God, by whom all things were created. I adore You. I earnestly beg You to come to me. Come to dwell in the place of Your choice, the Heart of Mary, the paradise of delights. She has adorned my soul with her virtues and her merits. I shall adore You as my beloved Brother in the arms of Your Mother. There I shall love You with all my heart.

To Mary:

Mary, my Mother, I am now about to become the sanctuary of Jesus. But what a poor dwelling I offer to the King of heaven. Receive Him in me and be to

Him a dwelling place. He finds His pleasure and delight wherever you are; even the stable of Bethlehem was delightful to Him because of your presence. Then He will also be pleased to take up His abode in my soul, if He finds His dear Mother there.

Come, dearest Mother, give me your pure loving Heart in place of mine, so cold and guilty. Adorn me with your virtues and merits and Jesus will find in my soul the perfect preparation which your soul offered Him at the moment of His Incarnation, and which He found there also after His ascension, when you received Him in Holy Communion. What happiness for me to be able to give you Jesus, the same gift the Heavenly Father gave you on the day of the Incarnation.

Immaculate Heart of Mary, I offer you Jesus, your Son, the King of angels and of men. Through Jesus and in Jesus, I wish to honor, love and thank you worthily for the many graces and mercies you have shown me during life.

Mary, lend me your heart, help me to love my God. Help me to prepare my poor heart to receive Jesus.

CONSECRATION OF THE HUMAN RACE TO THE SACRED HEART OF JESUS

Most Sweet Jesus, Redeemer of the human race, look down upon us humbly prostrate before Thy altar. We are Thine and Thine we wish to be; but to be more surely united with Thee, behold each one of us freely consecrates himself to-day to Thy Most Sacred Heart.

Many indeed have never known Thee; many, too, despising Thy precepts, have rejected Thee. Have mercy on them all, most merciful Jesus, and draw them to Thy Sacred Heart. Be Thou King, O Lord, not only of the faithful who have never forsaken Thee, but also of the prodigal children who have abandoned Thee. Grant that they may quickly return to their Father's house lest they die of wretchedness and hunger.

Be Thou King of those who are deceived by erroneous opinions, or whom discord keeps aloof, and call them back to the harbor of truth and unity of faith, so that soon there may be but one flock and one Shepherd.

Grant, O Lord, to Thy Church, assurance of freedom and immunity from harm; give peace and

45

freedom and immunity from harm; give peace and order to all nations, and make the earth resound, from pole to pole with one cry; Praise to the Divine Heart that wrought our salvation; to it be glory and honor forever. Amen

To Our Lady of the Most Blessed Sacrament

Virgin Mary, Our Lady of the Most Blessed Sacrament. Glory of the Chirstian People, Joy of the Universal Church, Salvation of the world, Pray for us and enkindle in the hearts of the faithful devotion to the most Holy Eucharist, that they may be worthy to receive Jesus daily. Our Lady of the Most Blessed Sacrament, pray for us.

("D")

THANKSGIVING

I thank You for all the favors You have given me. I give You thanks from the bottom of my heart for having created me; for all the joys of life, and its sorrows too; for the home You have given me; for the loved ones with which You have surrounded me; for the friends I have made through life.

My Lord God, I thank you for guarding me always, and keeping me safe; I thank you for forgiving me so often in the Sacrament of Reconciliation; for offering Yourself in the Holy Mass with all of your infinite merits to the Father for me; for coming to me in Holy Communion in spite of the coldness of my welcome; for your patient waiting in the adorable Sacrament of the altar.

My Jesus, I thank you for having lived, suffered, and died for me. I thank you for Your love. I thank You Lord, for preparing a place for me in heaven, where I hope to be happy with You and to thank You for all eternity. Amen.

"In everything give thanks" 1 Thess 5:18

PRAYER FOR THE TRIUMPH
OF THE CHURCH

O glorious St. Joseph, chosen to be the foster-father of Jesus, the chaste spouse of Mary ever Virgin, and the head of the Holy Family, and then appointed by the vicar of Christ to be the heavenly patron and defender of the church founded by Jesus, most confidently do I implore at this moment Thy powerful aid for all the church militant on earth. Do thou shield with Thy truly paternal love, especially the supreme pontiff and all the bishops and priests who are in union with the Holy See of Peter. Be the defender of all who labor for souls amidst the trials, the tribulation of this life, and cause all the peoples of the earth to submit themselves in the docile spirit to that church which is the ark of salvation for all men.

Be pleased also, dear Saint Joseph, to accept this dedication of myself which I now make unto thee. I dedicate myself wholly to thee, that thou mayest ever be my father, my patron, and my guide in the way of salvation.

Obtain for me great purity of heart and a fervent devotion to the interior life. Grant that, following thine example, I may direct all my actions to the greater glory of God, in union with the Sacred Heart of Jesus and the Immaculate Heart of Mary, and in union with thee.

Finally, pray for me, that I may be a partaker in the peace and joy which were thine at the hour of thy holy death. Amen.

PRAYER FOR VOCATIONS

O gentle God, You have called us to salvation and have sent Your Son to establish the Church for this purpose, and You have provided the Sacred Ministers.

The harvest is ever ready, but laborers are scarce. Inspire our youth to follow Jesus in the priesthood and in religious life. We ask this through Christ, Our Lord. Amen.

EMMAUS PRAYER FOR PRIESTS

Lord Jesus, hear our prayer
For the spiritual renewal of priests.
We praise You for giving their ministry to
    the church.
In these days, renew them with the gifts of
    Your Spirit.

You once opened the scriptures
To the disciples on the road to Emmaus.
Now renew Your ordained ministers
With the truth and the power of Your Word.
In Eucharist, You gave the Emmaus disciples
Renewed life and hope.
Nourish our priests with Your own Body and Blood.
Help them to imitate in their lives,
The death and resurrection they celebrate at
     Your altar.
Give priests enthusiasm for the Gospel,
Zeal for the salvation of all,
Courage in leadership,
Humility in service,
Fellowship with one another,
And with all their brothers and sisters in You.
For You love them, Lord Jesus,
And we love and pray for them in Your Name.
Amen

PRAYER FOR PRIESTS

O Jesus, Divine Master, I bless and thank Your most
loving heart for the institution of the priesthood.
The priests are sent by You, as You were sent by the
Father. To them, You have consigned the treasures
of Your doctrine, of Your law, of Your grace, and
souls themselves. Grant me the grace to love them,

to listen to them, and to let them guide me in Your ways. Send good laborers into Your vineyard, O Jesus. May the priests be the salt which purifies and preserves; may they be the light of the world; may they be the city placed on the mountain; may they all be made according to Your Heart; and may they have, one day in heaven, around themselves, as a crown of joy, a multitude of conquered souls.

≈≈

"The PRIESTHOOD is a masterpiece of Christ's Divine Love, wisdom and power."
"Never attack a PRIEST."
"Jesus and Mary, I love you, save PRIEST souls, convert souls. (Now asked by the Blessed Mother when speaking to Mirjana)"
" Oh Mary, Queen of the clergy, bring us good and Holy PRIESTS."

PRAYER OF ST. THOMAS MORE
(or another patron saint)

Give me the grace to long for Your Holy Sacraments, and especially to rejoice in the presence of Your Body, Sweet Savior Christ, in the Holy Sacrament of the altar. Amen.

CLOSING PRAYER

We leave this gathering with renewed spirit to continue our response throughout the week. Help us to pray with love and to persevere in our efforts to fast and sacrifice. Help us, also, day by day to understand more and more Your call to greater holiness and a life of joy by surrendering ourselves completely to God through Your Immaculate Heart.

We offer you our humble response to your call. We, in turn, thank You for leaving Your heavenly home to come as a loving mother to call us to peace, for teaching us the way and for being patient with our faltering efforts. We ask for Your guidance and for Your blessings. AMEN.

SONG
(*Tantum Ergo*)
or other suitable Eucharistic selection

BENEDICTION:
(Incensing Of The Blessed Sacrament During The Song)

Priest/Deacon: You have given them bread from Heaven,

ALL: Having all sweetness within it!

Priest/Deacon:
Lord, Our God, in this sacrament
We come into the presence of Jesus
Christ, Your Son, born of the Virgin Mary, and crucified for our salvation. May we who declare our faith in this fountain of love and mercy, drink from it the water of everlasting life. We ask this through Christ Our Lord. Amen

BLESSING OF THE PEOPLE WITH THE EUCHARIST

THE DIVINE PRAISES

Blessed be God.
Blessed be His Holy Name.
Blessed Be Jesus Christ, true
    God and true man.
Blessed be the Name of Jesus.
Blessed be His most Sacred
    Heart.
Blessed be His most Precious
    Blood.
Blessed be Jesus in the Most
    Holy Sacrament of the Altar.
Blessed be the Holy Spirit
    the Paraclete.
Blessed be the great Mother
    of God, Mary Most Holy.
Blessed be her holy and
    Immaculate Conception.
Blessed be her glorious
    Assumption.
Blessed be the name of Mary,
    Virgin and Mother.
Blessed be St. Joseph, her
    most chaste spouse.
Blessed be God, in His angels,
    and in His saints.

REPOSITION OF THE BLESSED SACRAMENT

ANNOUNCEMENTS

CLOSING SONG
(*Holy God*)
or other suitable selection

"My God and my all!"
"My Lord and my God!"
"Praised be Jesus Christ now and forever!"
"O Sacrament most holy, O Sacrament divine:
All praise and all thanksgiving be every
moment Thine!"

EUCHARIST PRAYER OF AKITA

Most Sacred Heart of Jesus, TRULY present in the Holy Eucharist, I consecrate my body and soul to be entirely one with Your heart, being sacrificed at every instant on all the altars of the world and giving praise to the Father, pleading for the coming of His kingdom.

Please receive this humble offering of myself. Use me as You will for the glory of the Father and the salvation of souls.

Most Holy Mother of God, never let me be separated from Your Divine Son. Please defend and protect me as Your special child. Amen

Exposition of the Blessed Sacrament

Prayer Before Mass and Holy Communion

Dear Jesus my Lord and my God, help me to realize that I received the most Holy Trinity into my soul and body at Baptism, and that at the Last Supper you gave me your Body and Blood as food for my soul.

I now come before you to prepare myself for the fruitful participation at Holy Mass and the worthy reception of Holy Communion. Help me to remember your presence within me, your presence among us who are here to pray and especially your presence in the Most Holy Eucharist. Give me a deep realization of your infinite love, mercy and forgiveness. Help me to be truly sorry and make reparations for my sins. As you forgave my sins and give me the Spirit of Repentance. Send the Holy Spirit to me and fill me with his gifts. Help me to focus my attention only on you so that I may adore, love and thank you. Without your help I can do none of these things.

I long to be able to pray in a deeper way, to realize the tremendous gift you have given in the Holy Eucharist, to appreciate your love and mercy and respond by giving you my heart, my life, my talents and my will. Fill me with a holy zeal for the extension of your kingdom here on earth, a kingdom of love, peace and joy.

Bless and help those around me, relatives, friends and all those who have no one to pray for them. Bless the priest who celebrates this Mass; give him a deep faith in your presence in the Holy Eucharist and call many to be zealous priests to serve your people. Amen.

Rev. Michael A. Walsh

RECONCILIATION PRAYERS
ADORATION PRAYERS

A. EXAMINATION OF CONSCIENCE

B. PSALM #51 (The Miserere; prayer of repentance)

C. ACTS OF CONTRITION

D. OTHER PRAYERS

PRAYER BEFORE CONFESSION

Come, Holy Spirit into my soul.

Enlighten my mind that I may know the sins I ought to confess, and grant me Your grace to confess them fully, humbly and with contrite heart. Help me to firmly resolve not to commit them again. O Blessed Virgin, Mother of my Redeemer, mirror of innocence and sanctity, and refuge of penitent sinners, intercede for me through the Passion of Your Son, that I may obtain the grace to make a good confession.

All you blessed Angels and Saints of God, pray for me, a most miserable sinner, that I may repent from my evil ways, that my heart may henceforth be forever united with Yours in eternal love. Amen

PSALM 51
THE MISERERE:
PRAYER OF REPENTANCE:

Have mercy on me, O God, in Your
goodness; in the greatness of Your
compassion wipe out my offense.
Thoroughly wash me from my guilt and
of my sin cleanse me.
For I acknowledge my offense, and my
sin is before me always:
"Against You only have I sinned, and
done what is evil in Your sight"
That You may be justified in Your
sentence, vindicated when You
condemn.
Indeed, in guilt was I born, and in sin
my mother conceived me;
Behold, You are pleased with sincerity
of heart, and in my inmost being You
teach me wisdom.
Cleanse me of sin with hyssop, that I
may be purified; wash me, and I shall
be whiter than snow.
Let me hear the sounds of joy and
gladness; the bones You have
crushed shall rejoice.

Turn away Your face from my sins, and
blot out all my guilt.
A clean heart create for me, O God,
and a steadfast spirit renew within me.
Cast me not out from Your presence,
and Your holy spirit take not from me.
Give me back the joy of Your
salvation, and a willing spirit sustain in me.
I will teach transgressors Your ways,
and sinners shall return to You.
Free me from blood guilt, O God, my
saving God; then my tongue shall
revel in Your justice.
O Lord, open my lips, and my mouth
shall proclaim Your praise.
For You are not pleased with
sacrifices; should I offer a holocaust, You would
not accept it.
My sacrifice, O God, is a contrite spirit;
a heart contrite and humbled, O God,
You will not spurn.
Be bountiful, O Lord, to Zion in Your
kindness by rebuilding the walls
of Jerusalem;
Then shall You be pleased with due
sacrifices, burnt offerings and
holocausts; then shall they offer up
bullocks on Your altar.

ACTS OF CONTRITION

1. "Father, I have sinned against You, and I am not worthy to be called Your child,. Be merciful to me, a sinner."

2. "Lord Jesus, Son of God, have mercy on me, a sinner."

3. "Dear Father, I know that You love me, and I love You, too. I am sorry for my sins. Please forgive me. I want to do good and to be like Your Son, Jesus. Help me to do the right things and to be good to everyone. Amen."

4. "My God, I am sorry for my sins with all my heart. In choosing to do wrong and failing to do good, I have sinned against You whom I should love above all things. I firmly intend, with Your help, to do penance, to sin no more, and to avoid whatever leads me to sin. Our Savior Jesus Christ suffered and died for us. In His name, my God, have mercy."

5. O my God, I am heartily sorry for having offended Thee, and I detest all my sins, because I dread the loss of heaven and the pains of hell.

But most of all because they offend Thee, my God, who art all-good and deserving of all my love. I firmly resolve, with the help of Thy grace, to confess my sins to do penance and to amend my life. Amen.

6. Lord God, I trust in Your goodness and mercy. I am sorry for all the wrong things I have done. I am sorry for all the good things I have not done. I want to love You with all my heart.

≈≈

Psalm 103 *"... The Lord is merciful and loving, slow to become angry and full of constant love. He does not keep on rebuking; he is not angry forever. He does not punish us as we deserve or repay us according to our sins and wrongs.*
As high as the sky is above the earth, so great is his love for those who have reverence for Him.
As far as the east is from the west, so far does he remove our sins from us...."

FORGIVENESS PRAYER **

Jesus,
I really do believe that You are the Son of God
and the Son of Mary, the true Christ
Who came into the world to save sinners.
And I admit that I am a sinner,
and that I need You.
Because without You I would have
been damned and lost forever.
So, with Mary as My Mother
and Teacher,
I want to magnify You as my Lord
and rejoice in You as my God and Savior,
My Jesus

So I open my heart to You right now
and from the arms of Mary I receive
You into my heart to be my personal Savior,
my very own Lord and Master.

Take over my life, and make me into the person
you want me to be.
Change me, teach me, protect me so that all my
thoughts and words and actions will be done
according to Your Spirit.

Thank You for dying on the cross for me,
and giving up Your Virgin-born Body
and Blood so that my sins are washed away and
no more remembered against me.
And thank You for promising You will never leave me
With the help of Your grace I will never leave you.

Thank You, Jesus.
Thank You Mary.
Amen.

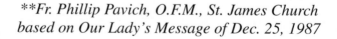

**Fr. Phillip Pavich, O.F.M., St. James Church
based on Our Lady's Message of Dec. 25, 1987

FIRST COMMANDMENT

I am the Lord, Thy God. Thou shalt not have strange gods before Me!

Have I willfully doubted or denied my holy religion? Have I consulted fortune tellers, or read forbidden books, or despaired of God's mercy? Have I neglected to worship God with prayer and the Mass?

SECOND COMMANDMENT

Thou shalt not take the name of the Lord, Thy God, in vain!

Have I made false, unlawful or unnecessary oaths? Have I taken God's name in vain?

THIRD COMMANDMENT

Remember Thou keep holy the Sabbath Day!

Have I absented myself without due cause from Mass on Sundays or Holydays of Obligation? Have I done unnecessary servile work on these days, or caused others to do so?

FOURTH COMMANDMENT

Honor Thy Father and Thy Mother!

Have I neglected my parents in their necessity? Have I been disobedient to them, or displayed anger toward them? Have I fulfilled my obligations toward my children? Instructed them? Reprimanded them when necessary? Watched over their companionships, etc.?

FIFTH COMMANDMENT

Thou shalt not kill!

Have I been angry? Have I been violent toward another, or caused violence without just cause? Have I been jealous of others?

SIXTH AND NINTH COMMANDMENTS

Thou shalt not commit adultery!
Thou shalt not covet Thy neighbor's wife!

Have I deliberately taken pleasure in impure thoughts? Have I committed any willful impure actions? Have I gone to places of amusement that I knew would lead me into sin? Have I kept away from other occasions of sin?

SEVENTH AND TENTH COMMANDMENTS

Thou shalt not steal!
Thou shalt not covet Thy neighbor's goods!

Have I stolen anything? Defrauded others in their just wages? Cheated in prices, weights, etc.? Have I through my own fault caused damage to the property of another? Have I made restitution for past sins of this nature? Have I now any ill-gotten goods?

EIGHTH COMMANDMENT

Thou shalt not bear false witness against
Thy neighbor!

Have I injured (without just cause) the name or reputation of another? By telling lies about him? By exposing without necessity his faults? Have I restored his good name when I have by untruth injured it?

69

EXAMINATION OF CONSCIENCE

1. Thank God for having preserved you through the past day.

2. Examine yourself as to the way you have conducted yourself through the day, in order to recall where and with whom you have been, and what you have done.

3. If you have done anything good, give thanks to God; if you have done anything amiss in thought, word, or deed, ask forgiveness for the sake of Jesus Christ, confessing the fault with real sorrow, and full determination to do better in the future.

4. Then commend your body and soul, the Church, your relatives and friends, to God. Ask God that his holy angels keep watch over you, and with God's blessing go to the rest he has appointed for you. Neither this practice nor that of the morning prayer should ever be omitted; by your morning prayer you open your soul's windows to the sunshine of righteousness, and by your evening devotions you close them against the shades of hell.

Saint Francis de Sales

PRAYER AFTER CONFESSION

My dearest Jesus,
I have told all my sins to the best of my ability. I have sincerely tried to make a good confession and I know that You have forgiven me. Thank You dear Jesus! Your divine heart is full of love and mercy for poor sinners. I love You dear Jesus; You are so good to me.
My loving Savior, I shall try to keep from sin and to love You more each day.
Dearest Mother Mary, pray for me and help me to keep all of my promises. Protect me and do not let me fall back into sin. Dear God, help me to lead a good life. Without Your grace I can do nothing.
Amen

Mother of God of Magadan

*"Jesus Meek and Humble of Heart,
Make My Heart Like Unto Thine"*

Used with permission of William Hart McNichols, S.J.

RECONCILIATION

MY CHILD:
I love you unconditionally.
I love you good or bad with no strings attached.
I love you like this because I know all about you.
I have known you ever since you were a child.
I know what I can do for you and
I know what I want to do for you.
I accept you.
I accept you just as you are.
You don't need to change yourself.
I'll do the changing when you are ready.
I love you just as you are.
Believe this, for I assure you it is true.
I care about you.
I care about every big and little thing which
    happens to you.
I care enough to do something about it.
Remember this.
I will help you when you need Me. Ask Me.
I love you. I accept you. I care about you.
I forgive you.
I forgive you and My forgiveness is complete.
It is not like that of humans who forgive but
    cannot forget.
I love you and My arms are open with love that asks.
    Please come here! Come here to Me.
I forgive you. Do not carry your guilt another moment.
    I carried it all for you on the Cross.
Believe this. It is true.

UNTITLED

There is nothing I can give you which you have not; But there is much, very much, that while I cannot give it, you can take.

No heaven can come to us unless our hearts find rest in today. Take heaven! No peace lies in the future which is not hidden in this present instant.

Take peace! The gloom of the world is but a shadow. Behind it, yet within reach, is joy.

There is radiance and glory in the darkness, could we but see, and to see, we have only to look. I beseech you to look. Life is so generous a giver, but we, judging its gifts by their covering, cast them away as ugly, or heavy, or hard.

Remove the covering, and you will find beneath it a living splendor, woven of love, by wisdom, with power. Welcome it, grasp it, and you touch the angel's hand that brings it to you. Everything we call a trial, a sorrow, or a duty, believe me, that angel's hand is there; the gift is there, and the wonder of an overshadowing presence.

Our joys too: be not content with them as joys. They, too, conceal more divine gifts. And so, at this time, I greet you. Not quite as the world sends greetings, but with profound esteem and with the prayer that for you now and forever, the day breaks, and the shadows flee away.

Fra. Giovanni 1513 A.D.

WHO IS JESUS CHRIST?

He was born in an obscure village the child of
a peasant woman.

He grew up in still another village, where
he worked in a carpenter shop until he
was 30. Then for three years he was an
itinerant preacher.

He never wrote a book

He never held an office.

He never had a family or owned a house.

He didn't go to college.

He never traveled 200 miles from the place where
he was born.

He did none of the things one usually associates
with greatness.

He had no credentials but himself.

He was only 33 when public opinion turned
against him.

His friends ran away.

He was turned over to his enemies and went
through the mockery of a trial.

He was nailed to a cross between two thieves.

While he was dying, his executioners gambled for
his clothing, the only property he had on earth.

When he was dead, he was laid in a borrowed grave
through the pity of a friend.

Nineteen centuries have come and gone, and today
he is the central figure of the human race, the
leader of mankind's progress.

All the armies that ever marched,
all the navies that ever sailed,
all the parliaments that ever sat,
all the kings that ever reigned,
put together,
have not affected
the life of man on earth
as much as that
One Solitary Life.

The Book of Life!

If you would like to know God, look at the Crucifix!
I you would like to LOVE GOD, LOOK AT
    the Crucifix!
If you want to serve God, look at the Crucifix!
If you wonder how much God loves you, look at
    the Crucifix!
If you wonder how much He wants you in heaven,
    look at the Crucifix!
If you wonder how He tries to prevent you from the
    yawning jaws of hell, look at the Crucifix!
If you wonder how much He will help you to save
    your immortal soul, look at the Crucifix!
If you wonder how much you should forgive others,
    look at the Crucifix!
If you wonder how much your faith demands of
    you, in humility, poverty, charity, meekness, and
    every virtue, look at the Crucifix!
If you want to know what unselfishness and gener-
    osity are, look at the Crucifix!
If you wonder how far your own unselfishness
    should go to bring others to Christ, look at
    the Crucifix!
If you want to understand the need for self-denial
    and mortification, look at the Crucifix!
If you wish to live well, look at the Crucifix!
If you wish to die well, look at the Crucifix!

BECAUSE OF YOUR
COMMITTED, ECSTATIC LOVE

...Praise you, Lord Jesus, for letting me crown you with thorns to take away our sins of pride. I give you permission to see and possess our sins of pride and drive the spirit of evil pride from our lives through, with and in the Holy Spirit and your eternal Truth. Praise you for urging us to see and possess your personal humility, honesty and wisdom through our Mother Mary, full of grace.

...Praise you, Lord Jesus, for letting me slap you in the face and even spit on it, to take away our sins of anger. I give you permission to see and possess our sins of anger and drive the spirit of evil anger from our lives through, with and in the Holy Spirit of your eternal Truth. Praise you for urging us to see and possess your personal patience, mercy and forgiveness through our Mother Mary, full of grace.

...Praise you, Lord Jesus, for letting me starve you, especially from water, to take away our sins of gluttony. I give you permission to see and possess our sins of gluttony and drive the evil spirit of gluttony from our lives through, with and in the Holy Spirit and your eternal Truth. Praise you for urging us to see and possess your personal temperance and sobriety, through our Mother Mary, full of grace.

...Praise you, Lord Jesus, for letting me strip you naked in public and beat your loins with whips, to take away our sins of lust. I give you permission to see and possess our sins of lust and drive the evil spirit of lust from our lives through, with and in the Holy Spirit and your eternal Truth. Praise you, for urging us to see and possess your personal chastity, purity and modesty through our Mother Mary.

...Praise you, Lord Jesus, for letting me drive nails through your hands to take away our sins of avarice. I give you permission to see and possess our sins of avarice and drive the evil spirit of avarice from our lives through, in and with the Holy Spirit and your eternal Truth. Praise you for urging us to see and possess your personal generosity, charity and poverty through our Mother Mary, full of grace.

...Praise you, Lord Jesus, for letting me drive nails through your feet to take away our sins of sloth. I give you permission to see and possess our sins of sloth and drive away the evil spirit of sloth through, with and in the Holy Spirit and your eternal Truth. Praise you for urging us to see and possess your personal fortitude, piety and fear of the Lord through our Mother Mary, full of grace.

...Praise you, Lord Jesus, for letting me beat your back so viciously that your bones are exposed, to take away our sins of envy. I give you permission to

79

see and possess our sins of envy and drive the evil spirit of envy from our lives through, with and in the Holy Spirit and your eternal Truth. Praise you for urging us to see and possess your personal faith and hope in the Father through our Mother Mary.

...Praise you, Lord Jesus, for letting me thrust a lance into your heart, to take away our sins of hatred for human life. I give you permission to see and possess our sins of hatred for human life and drive that evil spirit from our lives through, with and in the Holy Spirit and your eternal Truth. Praise you, for urging us to see and possess your personal love for human beings, through our Mother Mary, full of grace.

Lord Jesus, fill us ever more fully with your absolute fullness which you have after your Death, Resurrection and Ascension, sitting at the right hand of the Father. May your Holy Spirit, who fills Mary our Mother, fill each of us ever more.

Fr. C Mears Apr. 94

**Used with permission of Fr. Charles Mears

AN ANCIENT HOMILY
ON HOLY SATURDAY**

Something strange is happening - there is a great silence on earth today, a great silence and stillness. The whole earth keeps silence because the King is asleep. The earth trembled and is still because God has fallen asleep in the flesh and He has raised up all who have slept ever since the world began. God has died in the flesh and hell trembles with fear.

He has gone to search for our first parent, as for a lost sheep. Greatly desiring to visit those who live in darkness and in the shadow of death, He has gone to free from sorrow the captives Adam and Eve, He who is both God and the Son of Eve. The Lord approached them bearing the cross, the weapon that had won Him the victory. At the sight of Him, Adam, the first man He had created, struck his breast in terror and cried out to everyone: "My Lord be with you all." Christ answered and raised him up, saying: "Awake, O sleeper, and rise from the dead, and Christ will give you light."

I am your God, who for your sake have become your son. Out of love for you and for your descen-

** Used with permission. The English translation of "An Ancient Homily on Holy Saturday" from *The Liturgy of the Hours* © 1974, International Committee on English in the Liturgy, Inc. All rights reserved.

dants I now by my own authority command all who are held in bondage to come forth, all who are in darkness to be enlightened, all who are sleeping to arise. I order you, O sleeper, to awake. I did not create you to be held a prisoner in hell. Rise from the dead, for I am the life of the dead. Rise up, work of my hands, you who were created in My image. Rise, let us leave this place, for you are in Me and I am in you; together we form only one person and we cannot be separated.

For your sake I, your God, became your son; I, the Lord, took the form of a slave; I, whose home is above the heavens, descended to the earth and beneath the earth. For your sake, for the sake of man, I became like a man without help, free among the dead. For the sake of you, who left a garden, I was betrayed to the Jews in a garden, and I was crucified in a garden.

See on My face the spittle I received in order to restore to you the life I once breathed into you. See there the marks of the blows I received in order to refashion your warped nature in My image. On My back see the marks of the scourging I endured to remove the burden of sin that weighs upon your back. See My hands, nailed firmly to a tree, for you who once wickedly stretched out your hand to a tree.

I slept on the cross and a sword pierced My side for you who slept in paradise and brought forth Eve from your side. My side has healed the pain in yours. My sleep will rouse you from your sleep in hell. The sword that pierced Me has sheathed the sword that was turned against you.

Rise, let us leave this place. The enemy led you out of the earthly paradise. I will not restore you to that paradise, but I will enthrone you in heaven. I forbade you the tree that was only a symbol of life, but see, I who am life itself am now one with you. I appointed cherubim to guard you as slaves are guarded, but now I make them worship you as God. The throne formed by cherubim awaits you, its bearers swift and eager. The bridal chamber is adorned, the banquet is ready, the eternal dwelling places are prepared, the treasure houses of all good things lie open. The kingdom of heaven has been prepared for you from all eternity.

*Pope John Paul II performs the
Consecration of Russia on March 25th, 1984*

INDIVIDUAL AND/OR PRAYER GROUP PRAYERS

*Jesus, Son of God, have
Mercy on me, a sinner.*

PRAYER MEETING

OPENING PRAYER

Blessed be the Holy Trinity, One God, now and forever, Amen. Glory be to the Father who created me; glory be to the Son, who redeemed me; glory be to the Holy Spirit who sanctified me.

We have gathered here, Mary, Our Mother, Queen of Peace, because you have asked us to pray together for the conversion of sinners and peace in the world. We come with our hearts open for your love and guidance, so you may lead us to your Son, Jesus. Ask Him to send the Holy Spirit to enlighten us so we may understand your words and to strengthen us so we may have the courage to follow your directions.

The Apostles' Creed:

I believe in God, the Father Almighty, Creator of heaven and earth; and in Jesus Christ, His only Son, Our Lord; who was conceived by the Holy Spirit, born of the Virgin Mary, suffered under Pontius Pilate, was crucified, died and was buried; He descended into hell, the third day He arose from the dead; He ascended into heaven, sits at the right hand of God, the Father Almighty; from thence he shall come to judge the living and the dead. I believe in the Holy Spirit, the Holy Catholic Church, the communion of saints, the forgiveness of sins, the resurrection of the body and life everlasting. Amen.

Consecration to the Blessed Virgin

My Queen, my Mother, I give myself entirely to thee, and to show my devotion to thee, I consecrate to thee this day, my eyes, my ears, my mouth, my heart, my whole being without reserve. Wherefore good Mother as I am thine own, keep me, guard me, as thy property and possession. Amen

The Angelus

V. The Angel of the Lord declared unto Mary
R. And she conceived of the Holy Spirit (Hail Mary...)
V. Behold the handmaid of the Lord
R. Be it done unto me according to your Word (Hail Mary...)
V. And the Word was made flesh.
R. And dwelt among us (Hail Mary...)
V. Pray for us, O Holy Mother of God
R. That we may be made worthy of the promises of Christ.

Let us pray. Pour forth, we beseech You, O Lord, Your grace into our hearts, that we to whom the incarnation of Christ, Thy Son, was made known by the message of an angel, may by His passion and cross be brought to the glory of His resurrection, through the same Christ, Our Lord. Amen

PRAYER TO THE HOLY SPIRIT**

Come, Holy Spirit, enlighten my heart to see the things which are of God; Come, Holy Spirit, into my mind that I may know the things that are of God; Come, Holy Spirit, into my soul that I belong only to God; Sanctify all that I think, say and do, that all will be for the glory of God. Amen.

** Used with permission of Mark Miraville

CONSECRATION PRAYER

O Virgin Mary, most powerful Mother of Mercy, Queen of Heaven and Earth, in accordance with your wish made known at Fatima for your Triumph, I consecrate myself today to your Immaculate Heart. To you I entrust all that I have, all that I am. Reign over me, dearest Mother, that I may be yours in prosperity, in adversity, in joy and in sorrow, in health and in sickness, in life and in death.

Most compassionate Heart of Mary, Queen of Virgins, watch over my mind and heart and preserve me from the deluge of impurity which you lamented so sorrowfully at Fatima. I want to be pure like you. I want to atone for the many crimes committed against Jesus and you. I want to call down upon this country and the whole world, the peace of God in justice and charity.

Queen of the Most Holy Rosary and tender Mother of all people, I consecrate myself to you and to your Immaculate Heart, and recommend to you my family, my country, and the whole human race.

Please accept my consecration, dearest Mother, and use me as you wish, to accomplish your designs upon the world. O Immaculate Heart of Mary, rule over me and teach me how to allow the heart of Jesus to rule and triumph in me and around me as it has ruled and triumphed in you. Mindful of this consecration, I now promise to strive to imitate you each day by the practice of Christian virtues. Amen

DAILY RENEWAL OF THE CONSECRATION OF THE FAMILY TO THE MOST SACRED HEART OF JESUS

Most Sweet Jesus, humbly kneeling at Your feet, we renew the consecration of our family to Your divine heart. Be our King forever. In You we have full and entire confidence. May Your Spirit penetrate our thoughts, our desires, our words and our works. Bless our undertakings, share in our joys, in our trials, and in our labors. Grant us to know You better, to love You more and to serve You without faltering.

By the Immaculate Heart of Mary, Queen of Peace, set up Your kingdom in our country. Enter closely into the midst of our families and make them Your own by the solemn enthronement of Your Sacred Heart so that soon one cry may resound from home to home: May the Sacred Heart of Jesus and Immaculate Heart of Mary be loved, blessed, and glorified forever. Honor and glory be to the Sacred Hearts of Jesus and Mary. Sacred Heart of Jesus protect our families. Amen.

Divine Mercy Image
(COPYRIGHT 1982 MARIANS OF THE
IMMACULATE CONCEPTION)
Jesus I Trust In You "My Jesus Mercy"

91

THE CHAPLET OF DIVINE MERCY**
(using Rosary beads)

Begin: Our Father... Hail Mary...Glory Be...
The Apostles' Creed.
On the Large Beads:
"Eternal Father, I offer to You the Body and Blood, Soul and Divinity of Your dearly Beloved Son, our Lord Jesus Christ, in atonement for our sins and those of the whole world."
On the Small Beads:
"For the sake of His sorrowful Passion, have mercy on us and on the whole world."
Conclude with:
Holy God,
Holy Mighty One,
Holy Immortal One.
Have Mercy on us and on the wholeworld.
(3 times)

≈≈≈≈≈≈≈≈≈≈≈≈≈≈≈≈≈≈≈≈≈≈≈≈≈≈≈≈≈≈≈≈≈≈≈≈≈≈≈

"At three o'clock, implore My mercy, especially for sinners; and, if only for a brief moment, immerse yourself in My passion, particularly in My abandonment at the moment of agony. This is the hour of great mercy...In this hour I will refuse nothing to the soul that makes a request of Me in virtue of My Passion."

** "Taken from Divine Mercy in my Soul, the Diary of Blessed Faustina Kowalska, copyright 1987 Congregation of Marians. Printed with permission."

92

CLOSING PRAYER

Come Holy Spirit,
Replace the tension within us with a
 holy relaxation.
Replace the turbulence within us with a
 sacred calm.
Replace the anxiety within us with a
 quiet confidence.
Replace the fear within us with a strong faith.
Replace the bitterness within us with the
 sweetness of grace.
Replace the darkness within us with a gentle light.
Replace the coldness within us with a
 loving warmth.
Replace the night within us with Your day.
Replace the winter within us with Your spring.
Straighten our crookedness.
Mend our brokeness.
Fill our emptiness.
Dull the edge of our pride.
Sharpen the edge of our humility.
Light the fires of our love.
Quench the flame of our greed.
Let us see ourselves as You see us, that we might
see You as You have promised us. It is You who
calls us to this night and to Your work. It is You
who invites us to be Your hands and Your lips. As

we reflect upon Your word make us joyful messengers of Your good News and help us model ourselves so that our lives will convince others that true Christian joy is the result of giving ourselves into Your hands so that we might serve others. Amen.

"Indeed, everyone should painstakingly ready himself or herself for the apostolate, especially as an adult. For the advance of age brings with it better self-knowledge, thus enabling each person to evaluate more accurately the talents with which God has enriched every soul and to exercise more effectively those gifts which the Holy Spirit has bestowed on all for the good of others."

Decree on the Apostolate of the Laity,
Vatican Council II

MARY'S WAY OF THE CROSS**
Richard G. Furey, C.Ss.R.

Foreword

Is the Way of the Cross the way of every person's life? Doesn't every life have suffering, falls, hurts, rejections, condemnations, death, burial...and resurrection?

It has been a Catholic tradition through the centuries to meditate on the Way of the Cross, so that it becomes our way of life.

Mary, the Mother of Jesus, made that first way of the cross. These stations, called *Mary's Way of the Cross,* attempt to present that viewpoint. In these stations we see through Mary's eyes what Jesus was going through on the way to Calvary. Then we try to make practical applications to our lives.

These stations and these words are not the heart of the matter; the heart of the matter is to go deeper and deeper into the sufferings of Christ, so that we might come out of this spiritual journey with an appreciation of what Christ did for us, and a deeper love for him and for our brothers and sisters.

"We adore you, O Christ, and we praise you, because by your holy cross you have redeemed the world."

— Rev. Andrew Costello, C.Ss.R.

**These reflections and prayers are reprinted with permission from *Mary's Way of the Cross,* by Richard Furley, copyright 1984 by Redemptorist Fathers and Brothers, and published by Twenty-Third Publications, P.O. Box 180, Mystic, CT 06355. (800) 321-0411.

95

FIRST STATION

*"We adore you, O Christ, and we praise you,
because by your holy cross you have
redeemed the world."*

JESUS IS CONDEMNED TO DIE

It was early Friday morning
when I saw my son.
That was the first glimpse I had of him
since they took him away.
His bruised and bleeding skin
sent a sword of pain deep into my heart
and tears down my cheeks.
Then Pilate, from his chair of judgment,
asked the crowd why they wanted my son executed.
All around me they shouted.
"Crucify him!"
I wanted to plead with them to stop,
but I knew this had to be.
So I stood by and cried silently.

Lord Jesus,
it is hard for me to imagine
the anguish your mother felt
at your condemnation.
But what about today, when I hold a grudge...?

"Crucify him!"
"When I judge others...?
"Crucify him!"
Doesn't this bring tears of anguish
to both you and your mother?
Forgive me, Jesus.

SECOND STATION

"We adore you, O Christ, and we praise you,
because by your holy cross you have
redeemed the world."

JESUS TAKES HIS CROSS

Regaining a little strength,
I walked with the crowds
to the entrance of the square.
A door flew open
and my son stumbled out,
the guards laughing behind him.
Two men dragged over a heavy wooden cross
and dropped it on his shoulders.
Then they shoved him down the road.
My pain for him was unbearable.
I wanted to take the cross from him
and carry it myself.
But I knew this had to be,
so I walked on silently.

Lord Jesus, I beg you to forgive me
for the many times
I have added more weight to your cross
by closing my eyes
to the pain and loneliness of my neighbor.

Forgive me for gossiping about others
and for always trying to find excuses
to avoid certain people
who wish to talk with me.
Help me to be like Mary,
always seeking to lighten the crosses of others.
Forgive me, Jesus.

THIRD STATION

"We adore you, O Christ, and we praise you, because by your holy cross you have redeemed the world."

JESUS FALLS THE FIRST TIME

I followed close behind my son
as he stumbled toward Calvary.
Nothing had ever hurt me more
than to see him in such pain.
I saw the cross digging into his shoulders.
My heart dropped when I saw him fall
face to the ground,
the heavy cross landing squarely on his back. For a
moment I thought my beloved son was dead. Now,
my whole body began to tremble. Then the guards
kicked him.
He rose slowly and began to walk again,
yet they still whipped him. I wanted to protect him
with my own body. But, I knew this had to be, so I
walked on and wept silently.

Lord, how often have I seen you fall,
and, unlike Mary, have left you there
without concern?
How often have I seen people make mistakes

and laughed at them?
How often do I find myself getting angry
when someone does things differently than I?
Mary offered you her support
through your entire passion.
Help me to do the same for you
by the support I give to others.
Lord, have mercy on me.

FOURTH STATION

"We adore you, O Christ, and we praise you,
because by your holy cross you have
redeemed the world."

JESUS MEETS HIS GRIEVING MOTHER

I had managed to break through the crowd
and was walking side by side with my son.
I called to him through the shouting voices.
He stopped.
Our eyes met,
mine full of tears of anguish,
his full of pain and confusion.
I felt helpless;
then his eyes said to me,
"Courage! There is a purpose for this."
As he stumbled on, I knew he was right.
So I followed and prayed silently.

Lord Jesus,
forgive me the many times
our eyes met and I turned mine away.
Forgive me the times
things did not go my way
and I let everyone know about it.
Forgive me the times

I brooded over little inconveniences
or became discouraged
and did not heed your call to courage!
Yes, Lord,
our eyes have met many times,
but fruitlessly.

FIFTH STATION

SIMON HELPS JESUS CARRY HIS CROSS

I could now see almost complete helplessness
on the face of my son
as he tried to carry his heavy load.
Each step looked as if it would be his last.
I felt his every pain in my heart
and I wanted the whole thing to end.
Then I noticed some commotion near Jesus.
The guards had pulled a protesting man
from the crowd.
They forced him to pick up the back of the cross
to help lighten my son's load.
He asked the guards why this had to be.
I knew,
and so followed silently.

Lord Jesus,
I have many times
refused to help you.
I have been a selfish person
who has often questioned your word.

Don't let me remain like Simon,
but help me to be like your mother, Mary,
who always silently followed and obeyed.

SIXTH STATION

*"We adore you, O Christ, and we praise you,
because by your holy cross you have
redeemed the world."*

VERONICA WIPES THE FACE OF JESUS

As I continued close by Jesus,
a woman pushed past the guards,
took off her veil
and began to wipe my son's sweating, bloody face.
The guards immediately pulled her back.
Her face seemed to say,
"Why are you doing this to him?"
I knew,
so I walked on in faith, silently.

Lord,
this woman gave you the best she could.
On the other hand,
I have wanted to take more than I give.
So many opportunities arise every day
for me to give to you
by giving to others-
but I pass them by.
My Savior,
never let me ask why again,
but help me to give all I have to you.

106

SEVENTH STATION

"We adore you, O Christ, and we praise you,
because by your holy cross you have
redeemed the world."

JESUS FALLS THE SECOND TIME

Again
my son fell,
and again my grief was overwhelming
at the thought that he might die.
I started to move toward him,
but the soldiers prevented me.
He rose and stumbled ahead slowly.
Seeing my son fall,
get up again,
and continue on,
was bitter anguish to me.
But, since I knew this had to be.
I walked on silently.

Lord,
of all people
Mary was your most faithful follower,
never stopping in spite of all the pain she felt
for you.

I have many times turned away from you
by my sins
and have caused others to turn away from you.
I beg you to have mercy on me.

EIGHTH STATION

"We adore you, O Christ, and we praise you,
because by your holy cross you have
redeemed the world."

JESUS SPEAKS TO THE WOMEN

I was walking a few steps behind Jesus
when I saw him stop.
Some women were there
crying for him and pitying him.
He told them not to shed tears for him.
They had the opportunity to accept him
as the messiah;
like many others, they rejected him instead.
He told them to shed tears for themselves,
tears that would bring their conversion.
They did not see the connection between that
and his walk to death.
I did, and as he walked on, I followed silently.

My Savior,
many times have I acted like these women,
always seeing the faults of others
and pitying them.
Yet, very rarely have I seen my own sinfulness

109

and asked your pardon.
Lord, you have taught me through these women.
Forgive me, Lord,
for my blindness.

NINTH STATION

"We adore you, O Christ, and we praise you,
because by your holy cross you have
redeemed the world."

JESUS FALLS THE THIRD TIME

This fall of Jesus was agony to me.
Not only had he fallen on the rocky ground again,
but now he was almost at the top of the hill
of crucifixion.
The soldiers screamed at him and abused him,
almost dragging him the last few steps.
My heart pounded
as I imagined what they would do to him next.
But, I knew this had to be,
so I climbed the hill silently behind him.

My loving Jesus,
I know that many times
I have offered my hand to help people
but when it became inconvenient
or painful to me
I left them,
making excuses for myself.
Help me, Lord,
to be like your mother, Mary,
and never take my supporting hand
away from those who need it.

111

TENTH STATION

*"We adore you, O Christ, and we praise you,
because by your holy cross you have
redeemed the world."*

JESUS IS STRIPPED OF HIS GARMENT

With my son finally relieved
of the weight of the cross.
I thought he would have a chance to rest.
But the guards immediately started
to rip his clothes
off his blood-clotted skin.
The sight of my son in such pain
was unbearable.
Yet, since I knew this had to be.
I stood by and cried silently.

Lord,
in my own way I too have stripped you.
I have taken away the good name of another
by foolish talk,
and have stripped people of human dignity
by my prejudice.
Jesus,
there are so many ways I have offended you
through the hurt I have caused others.
Help me to see you in all people.

ELEVENTH STATION

*"We adore you, O Christ, and we praise you,
because by your holy cross you have
redeemed the world."*

JESUS IS NAILED TO THE CROSS

As they threw Jesus on the cross,
he willingly allowed himself to be nailed.
As they punctured his hands and his feet
I felt the pain in my heart.
Then they lifted up the cross.
There he was, my son,
whom I love so much,
being scorned as he struggled
for the last few moments of earthly life.
But I knew this had to be,
so I stood by and prayed silently.

Lord,
what pain you endured for me.
And what pain your mother went through,
seeing her only son die for love of me!
Yet, both you and she are ready
to forgive me
as soon as I repent of my sin.
Help me, Lord,
to turn away from my sinfulness.

TWELFTH STATION

"We adore you, O Christ, and we praise you,
because by your holy cross you have
redeemed the world."

JESUS DIES ON THE CROSS

What greater pain is there for a mother
than to see her son die right before her eyes!
I, who had brought this savior into the world
and watched him grow,
stood helplessly beneath his cross
as he lowered his head
and died.
His earthly anguish was finished, but mine was
greater than ever.
Yet, this had to be
and I had to accept it,
so I stood by and I mourned silently.

My Jesus,
have mercy on me
for what my sins have done to you
and to others.
I thank you for your great act of love.
You have said

114

that true love is laying down your life
for your friends.
Let me always be your friend.
Teach me to live my life for others,
and not fail you again.

THIRTEENTH STATION

*"We adore you, O Christ, and we praise you,
because by your holy cross you have
redeemed the world."*

JESUS IS TAKEN FROM THE CROSS

The crowd had gone;
the noise had stopped
I stood quietly with one of Jesus' friends
and looked up at the dead body
of our savior,
my son.
Then two men took the body from the cross
and placed it in my arms.
A deep sorrow engulfed my being.
Yet, I also felt
deep joy.
Life had ended cruelly for my son,
but it had also brought life to all of us.
I knew this had to be,
and I prayed silently.

Lord,
your passion has ended.
Yet, it still goes on
whenever I choose sin over you.

I have done my part in your crucifixion
and now, my savior,
I beg your forgiveness with all my heart.
Help me to live a life
worthy of you and your mother.

FOURTEENTH STATION

"We adore you, O Christ, and we praise you, because by your holy cross you have redeemed the world."

JESUS IS PLACED IN THE TOMB

We brought Jesus' body to a tomb
and I arranged it there myself,
silently weeping,
silently rejoicing.
I took one more look at my loving son,
and then walked out.
They closed the tomb
and before I left, I thought,
I knew this had to be...
it had to be for you!
I would wait in faith
silently.

Yes, my Lord,
this had to be
because you love me, and for no other reason.
All you ask is that I live a good life.
You never said such a life
would be easy.
I am willing to leave sin behind
and live for you alone,
in my brothers and sisters.

118

FIFTEENTH STATION

*"We adore you, O Christ, and we praise you,
because by your holy cross you have
redeemed the world."*

JESUS IS RAISED FROM THE DEAD

I could only be most grateful
for the sacrifice of my son for us.
Yet, what emptiness I felt
trying to live without him whom I loved so!
But, only two days later
that emptiness was filled beyond belief—
he had risen!
Our savior had opened the doors
to a new life.
That is the way it had to be—
because his undying love for you
would not stop at anything less.
I could rejoice forever,
but not in silence.

My Savior,
thank you!
Thank you for such endless love
that helps me to rise
out of my own sinfulness.

119

I will try again
to live a better life.
Help me to always remember that love.
Mary, mother of our risen Savior,
teach me to be like you,
and in my love for others,
love him in return.

STABAT MATER

At the Cross her station keeping,
Stood the mournful Mother weeping,
Close to Jesus to the last.

(1)
Through her heart, His sorrow sharing,
All His bitter anguish bearing,
Now, at length, the sword has passed.

(2)
O, how sad and sore distressed
Was that Mother highly blessed
Of the sole Begotten One.

(3)
Christ above in torment hangs
She beneath beholds the pangs
Of her dying, glorious Son.

(4)
Is there one who would not weep,
Whelmed in miseries so deep
Christ's dear Mother to behold?

(5)
Can the human heart refrain
From partaking in her pain,
In that Mother's pain untold?

121

(6)

Bruised, derided, cursed, defiled
She beheld her tender Child,
All with bloody scourges rent.

(7)

For the sins of His own nation
Saw Him hang in desolation
Till His spirit forth He sent.

(8)

O sweet Mother! Fount of Love,
Touch my spirit from above
Make my heart with yours accord.

(9)

Make me feel as You have felt
Make my soul to glow and melt
With the love of Christ, my Lord.

(10)

Holy Mother, pierce me through;
In my heart each wound renew
Of my Savior crucified.

(11)

Let me share with you His pain
Who for all my sins was slain,
Who for me in torments died.

122

(12)
Let me mingle tears with thee
Mourning Him who mourned for me,
All the days that I may live.

(13)
By the cross with you to stay
There with you to weep and pray
Is all I ask of you to give.

(14)
Virgin of all virgins blest!
Listen to my fond request;
Let me share thy grief divine.

MEDITATION FROM AN ANCIENT FLEMISH CALVARY

I am the Light, and you do not see me
I am the Way, and you do not follow me
I am the Truth, and you do not believe me.
I am the Life, and you do not seek me.
I am the Master, and you do not listen to me.
I am the Chief, and you do not obey.
I am your God, and you do not pray to me.
I am the Best Friend, and you do not love me.

If you are unhappy, do not blame me!

Mother Teresa gave her sisters the following rules to follow in order to practice humility...

Speak as little as possible about yourself;
Keep busy with your own affairs and not those
    of others;
Avoid curiosity;
Do not interfere in the affairs of others;
Accept small irritations with good humor;
Do not dwell on the faults of others;
Accept censures even if unmerited;
Give in to the will of others;
Accept insults and injuries;

Accept contempt, being forgotten and disregarded:
Accept injuries and insults;
Be courteous and delicate even when provoked by
someone;
Do not seek to be admired and loved;
Do not protect yourself behind your own dignity;
Give in, in discussions, even when you are right;
Choose always the more difficult task.

Prayer Before Bedtime

Now I lay me down to sleep
and pray my soul the Lord to keep.
If I die before I wake,
I pray my soul the Lord will take.

REGINA COELI

O Queen of heaven, rejoice! Alleluia.
For He whom you did merit to bear, Alleluia.
He has risen, as He said, Alleluia.
Pray for us to God, Alleluia.
   V. Rejoice and be glad, O Virgin Mary, Alleluia.
   R. For the Lord has risen indeed. Alleluia.

LET US PRAY

O God, Who by the resurrection of Your Son,
Our Lord Jesus Christ, has given joy to the whole
world, grant, we beseech You, that through the
intercession of the Virgin Mary, His Mother, we
may attain the same joys of eternal life. Through the
same Christ Our Lord. Amen

COME, HOLY SPIRIT

Come, Holy Spirit, fill the hearts of Your faithful
and enkindle in them the fire of Your love.
Send forth Your Spirit and they shall be created and
You shall renew the face of the earth.
O God, who has instructed the hearts of Your faithful by the light of the Holy Spirit, grant that by the
same Holy Spirit we may have a right judgment in
all things and evermore rejoice in His consolations.
Through Christ Our Lord. Amen

GENERAL PRAYERS

"Pray Without Ceasing"
1 Thess. 5:17

LIFE IS FRAGILE HANDLE IT WITH CARE

"GOD GOVERNS THE WORLD BUT PRAYER GOVERNS GOD."

STEPS FOR PRAYING

> **A**doration
> **C**ontrition
> **T**hanksgiving
> **S**upplication

≈≈

WHY WERE THE SAINTS SAINTS?

Because they were:
>   Cheerful, ... when it was hard to be cheerful;
>   Patient, ... when it was difficult to be patient;
>   Agreeable, ... when they wanted to disagree;
>   Silent, ... when they wanted to criticize;

Because they pushed ahead when they wanted to stand still.

127

PRELUDE TO PRAYER

You do not have to be clever to please Me; all you have to do is want to love Me. Just speak to Me as you would to anyone of whom you are very fond. Are there any people you want to pray for? Say their names to Me, and ask of Me as much as you like. I am generous, and know all their needs, but I want you to show your love for them and Me by trusting Me to do what I know is best.

Tell me about the poor, the sick, and the sinners, and if you have lost the friendship or affection of anyone, tell Me about that too.

Is there anything you want for your soul? If you like, you can write out a long list of all your needs, and come and read it to Me. Tell Me of the things you feel guilty about. I will forgive you if you will accept it.

Just tell Me about your pride, your touchiness, self-centeredness, meanness and laziness. I still love you in spite of these. Do not be ashamed; there are many saints in heaven who had the same faults as you; they prayed to Me, and little by little, their faults were corrected.

Do not hesitate to ask Me for blessings for the body and mind; for health, memory, and success. I can give everything, and I always do give everything needed to make souls holier for those who truly want it.

What is it that you want today? Tell Me, for I long to do you good. What are your plans? Tell Me about them. Is there anyone you want to please? What do you want to do for them?

And don't you want to do anything for Me? Don't you want to do a little good to the souls of your friends who perhaps have forgotten Me? Tell Me about your failures, and I will show you the cause of them. What are your worries? Who has caused you pain? Tell Me all about it and add that you will forgive, and be kind to him, and I will bless you. Are you afraid of anything? Have you any tormenting, unreasonable fears? Trust yourself to Me. I am here. I see everything. I will not leave you.

Have you no joys to tell Me about? Why do you not share your happiness with Me? Tell Me what has happened since yesterday to cheer and comfort you. Whatever it was, however big, however small, I prepared it. Show Me your gratitude and thank Me. Are temptations bearing heavily upon you? Yielding to temptations always disturbs the peace of your soul. Ask Me, and I will help you overcome them. Well, go along now. Get on with your work or play, or other interests. Try to be quieter, humbler, more submissive, kinder; and come back soon and bring Me a more devoted heart. Tomorrow I shall have more blessings for you.

Anonymous

129

PRAYER FOR TODAY

O my God, this day in my prayers, I pray for:

— For all families to pray together
— My spouse and my children
— For all the youth of the world
— My mother and father
— My grandparents
— My brothers, sisters, relatives and all friends
— For all those who have no one to pray for them
— The Holy Father and all his intentions and his safety
— All bishops, priests, brothers and sisters
— Mother Church and all her children
— The poor souls in purgatory
— All those for whom I have promised to pray
— Those who love me and those who hate me
— The dying and those who die today
— The sick, the poor, the rich
— For the homeless that they find shelter and food
— The neglected, the persecuted, and the enslaved
— Those endangered and in distress
— The tempted, the doubting, the despairing
— My country, its president, and all its officials
— Those who died in military service for their country

- Those who lost loved ones in the struggle
- For all nations and all races
- For peace in the world and all its people
- To end all ABORTIONS
- Men of good will that they may come to the fullness of the faith
- Men of evil ways that they may be converted
- For all those called to serve in the Mission
- That all will respond to the request for a global consecration
- For the Triumph of the Immaculate Heart of Mary
- For the Reign of the Sacred Heart of Jesus

≈≈

("Maranatha") "Come Lord Jesus" (Rev 22.20)

≈≈

"WHO IS LIKE UNTO GOD!"

≈≈

CONFITEOR

I confess to Almighty God, to Blessed Mary ever Virgin, to blessed Michael the Archangel, to blessed John the Baptist, to the holy Apostles Peter and Paul, to all the saints, and to you, Father, that I have sinned exceedingly in thought, word and deed, through my fault, through my fault, through my most grievous fault. Therefore I beseech blessed Mary ever Virgin, blessed Michael the Archangel, blessed John the Baptist, the holy Apostles Peter and Paul, all the saints, and you, Father, to pray to the Lord our God for me.

P. May almighty God have mercy on me, forgive me my sins, and bring me to life everlasting.
R. Amen.

PRAYER BEFORE THE CRUCIFIX

Behold, O kind and gentle Jesus, I kneel before You and pray that You would impress upon my heart the virtues of faith, hope and charity, with true repentance for my sins and a firm purpose of amendment. At the same time, with sorrow I meditate on Your five precious wounds, having in mind the words which David spoke in prophecy: "They have pierced My Hands and My Feet; they have numbered all My Bones."

ANIMA CHRISTI

Soul of Christ, sanctify me; Body of Christ, save me; Blood of Christ, inebriate me; Water from the side of Christ, wash me; Passion of Christ, strengthen me; O good Jesus, hear me; Within Your wounds hide me; Separated from You, let me never be; From the evil one protect me; At the hour of my death, call me; And close to You bid me; That with Your saints, I may be, praising You forever and ever. Amen

THE MEMORARE

Remember, O most gracious Virgin Mary, that never was it known that anyone who fled to your protection, implored your help, or sought your intercession, was left unaided. Inspired by this confidence, I fly unto you, O Virgin of virgins, my Mother. To you I come; before you I stand sinful and sorrowful. O Mother of the Word Incarnate! Despise not my petitions, but in your mercy hear and answer me. Amen.

"Jesus, Mary and Joseph, I love you very much. I beg you to spare the life of the unborn baby that I have spiritually adopted, who is in danger of abortion."

OUR LADY OF GUADALUPE
"Am I not here, I who am your Mother?"

PRAYER TO END ABORTIONS

Mother Mary, as you carried your Divine Child in your womb you rejoiced and glorified the Lord. Touch with pity the hearts of those women pregnant in our world today who think of murder, not motherhood. Help them to see that the child they carry is made in God's image—as well as theirs—made for eternal life. Dispel their fear and selfishness and give them true womanly hearts to love their babies and give them birth and all the needed care that a mother alone can give. Mary, Mother of Christ, show us all, one day the blessed fruit of your womb, Jesus. *(Mother Teresa says, " that abortion kills two; the baby and the conscience of the mother.")*

PRAYER FOR HEALING

Lord, You invite all who are burdened to come to You. Allow Your healing hand to heal me. Touch my soul with Your compassion for others. Touch my heart with Your courage and infinite love for all. Touch my mind with Your wisdom, that my mouth may always proclaim Your praise. Teach me to reach out to You in my need, and help me to lead others to You by my example. Most loving Heart of Jesus, bring me health in body and spirit that I may serve You with all my strength. Touch gently this life which You have created, now and forever. Amen.

MORNING OFFERING:

O Jesus, through the Immaculate Heart of Mary, I offer You my prayers, works, joys and sufferings of this day in union with the Holy Sacrifice of the Mass throughout the world. I offer them for all the intentions of Your Sacred Heart: the salvation of souls, reparation for sin, the reunion of all Christians. I offer them for the intentions of our Bishops and of all members of the Apostleship of Prayer, and in particular for those recommended by our Holy Father this month.

EVENING PRAYER

Watch, O Lord, with those who wake, or watch, or weep tonight, and give Your Angels and Saints charge over those who sleep. Tend Your sick ones, O Lord Christ, Rest Your weary ones, Bless Your dying ones, Soothe Your suffering ones, Pity Your afflicted ones, Shield Your joyous ones, And all for Your love's sake. Amen

(St. Augustine)

MAGNIFICAT

My soul magnifies the Lord, and my spirit rejoices in God my Savior; Because He has regarded the lowliness of His handmaid; for, behold, henceforth all generations shall call me Blessed; because He who is mighty has done great things for me, and holy is His name;

And His mercy is from generation to generation on those who fear Him. He has shown might with His arm, He has scattered the proud in the conceit of their heart. He has put down the mighty from their thrones, and has exalted the lowly. He has filled the hungry with good things, and the rich He has sent away empty. He has given help to Israel, His servant, mindful of his mercy. Even as He spoke to our fathers —to Abraham and to His posterity forever.

THE KEY TO THE IMMACULATE HEART OF MARY

O Mary, Protectress of the Faith, hear our prayer - and ask Your beloved Son to receive our Faith into His Sacred Hands; ask Him to hide our Faith in His Wounds and protect it from all evil. Amen.

ACT OF FAITH

O my God, I firmly believe that You are one God in
three divine Persons, Father, Son, and Holy Spirit. I
believe that Your divine Son became man, died for
our sins, and that He will come to judge the living
and the dead. I believe these and all the truths which
the Holy Catholic Church teaches, because You
have revealed them, who can neither deceive nor
be deceived.

ACT OF HOPE

O my God, relying on Your almighty power and
infinite mercy and promises, I hope to obtain pardon
of my sins, the help of Your grace, and life everlasting through the merits of Jesus Christ, my Lord
and Redeemer.

ACT OF LOVE

O my God, I love You above all things, with my
whole heart and soul, because You are all-good and
worthy of all love. I love my neighbor as myself for
the love of You. I forgive all who have injured me,
and ask pardon of all whom I have injured. Amen.

JESUS PRAYER

O My Jesus, I adore thee in the most Holy Sacrament of the altar, I acknowledge Thee as my creator and sovereign Lord, in deepest humility, I prostrate myself before Thee, bless me O my Savior and suffer me to abide with Thee for all eternity. Amen

PRAYER FOR A HAPPY DEATH

Joseph, foster-father of Jesus, most pure spouse of the Virgin Mary, pray for us daily to the same Jesus, the Son of God, that we, being defended by the power of His grace and striving faithfully in life, may be crowned by Him at the hour of death.

PRAYER TO ST. JOSEPH

O Joseph, Holy Guardian of Jesus and Mary, assist us by Thy prayers in all the necessities of life. Ask of Jesus that special grace, which He granted to thee, to watch over our home at the pillow of the sick and dying, so that with Mary and with thee, Heaven may find our family unbroken in the Sacred Heart of Jesus. Amen.

ST. JOSEPH, PROTECTOR OF HOMES

St. Joseph, protect our home. Pour forth heaven's blessings on our family. Remain in our midst. Help us to live in love and harmony, in peace and joy. May the wholesome fear of God strengthen us that virtue may adorn what we do and our way may lead to heaven.
"To you this day I give the key to our dwelling place. Lock out all things that could do us harm. Lock my home and my loved ones with me in the hearts of Jesus and Mary. This I beg of you that our days may be like your days in the holy home at Nazareth. Amen."

GOLDEN ARROW PRAYER

May the most holy, most sacred, most adorable, most mysterious and unutterable Name of God be always praised, blessed, loved, adored and glorified in heaven on earth and under the earth, by all the creatures of God, and by the Sacred Heart of our Lord Jesus Christ in the most Holy Sacrament of the altar.

Our Lord told a Carmelite Nun, "This Golden Arrow will wound My Heart delightfully, and heal the wounds inflicted by blasphemy."

140

PRAYER FOR THE SOULS IN PURGATORY

O gentle Heart of Jesus, ever present in the Blessed Sacrament, ever consumed with burning love for the poor captive souls in Purgatory, have mercy on them.
Be not severe in Your judgments, but let some drops of Your Precious Blood fall upon the devouring flames.
And, Merciful Savior, send Your angels to conduct them to a place of refreshment, light and peace. Amen.

FOR POOR SOULS

Eternal rest grant unto them O Lord.
R. And let perpetual light shine upon them
May their souls and the souls of the faithful departed, through the mercy of God, rest in peace. Amen

"It is therefore a holy and wholesome thought to pray for the dead, that they may be loosed from their sins."

2 Maccabees 12:46

"I tell you that you shall not come out from there until you have paid the very last penny."

St. Matthew 5:26

141

Eternal Father I offer thee the Most Precious Blood of Thy Divine Son Jesus, in union with the masses said throughout the world today, for all of the holy souls in purgatory.

(St. Gertrude the Great was told by Our Lord that the above prayer would release a 1000 souls from purgatory each time it is said.)

BEATITUDES

Blessed are the poor in spirit,
 for theirs is the kingdom of heaven.
Blessed are the meek,
 for they shall possess the earth.
Blessed are they who mourn,
 for they shall be comforted.
Blessed are they who hunger and thirst for
    justice, for they shall be satisfied.
Blessed are the clean of heart,
 for they shall see God.
Blessed are the peacemakers,
 for they shall be called children of God.
Blessed are they who suffer persecution for
    justice' sake, for theirs is the kingdom
of heaven.
Blessed are you when men reproach you, and
    persecute you, and speaking falsely, say all
manner of evil against you, for my sake.

SACRAMENTS

Baptism, Confirmation, Holy Eucharist, Penance, Extreme Unction, Holy Orders, and Matrimony (What is a sacrament? A sacrament is an outward sign instituted by Christ to give grace.)

CORPORAL WORKS OF MERCY
1. To feed the hungry.
2. To give drink to the thirsty.
3. To clothe the naked.
4. To visit the imprisoned.
5. To shelter the homeless.
6. To visit the sick.
7. To bury the dead.

SPIRITUAL WORKS OF MERCY
1. To admonish the sinner.
2. To instruct the ignorant.
3. To counsel the doubtful.
4. To comfort the sorrowful.
5. To bear wrongs patiently.
6. To forgive all injuries.
7. To pray for the living and the dead.

THE TEN COMMANDMENTS

(1) I am the Lord Thy God; thou shalt not have strange gods before me.

(2) Thou shalt not take the name of the Lord Thy God in vain.

(3) Remember thou keep holy the Lord's day.

(4) Honor Thy father and Thy mother.

(5) Thou shalt not kill.

(6) Thou shalt not commit adultery.

(7) Thou shalt not steal.

(8) Thou shalt not bear false witness against thy neighbor.

(9) Thou shalt not covet thy neighbor's wife.

(10) Thou shalt not covet thy neighbor's goods.

PSALM 19:7-11
The Law of the Lord is perfect

GOD'S TWO GREAT COMMANDMENTS

The basis of all law (your rule of life) rests on two commandments: "You shall love the Lord, your God, with all your heart, with all your soul, and with all your mind....You shall love your neighbor as yourself" (Matthew 22:37,39)

≈≈

SEVEN DEADLY SINS
Pride, Covetousness, Lust, Anger, Gluttony, Envy and Sloth.

THEOLOGICAL VIRTUES
Faith, Hope and Charity

CARDINAL / *MORAL* VIRTUES
Prudence, Justice, Fortitude, and Temperance (Filial Piety, Obedience, Veracity, Liberality, Patience, Humility, Chastity, Purity)

THE LAST THINGS
Death, Judgment, Heven and Hell.

VENI CREATOR

Come, O creator Spirit blest!
And in our souls take up thy rest;
Come with Thy grace and heavenly aid,
To fill the hearts which Thou hast made.

Great Paraclete! To Thee we cry,
O highest gift of God most high!
O font of life! O fire of love!
And sweet anointing from above.

Thou in Thy sevenfold gifts art known,
The finger of God's hand we own;
The promise of the Father, Thou!
Who dost the tongue with power endow.

Kindle our senses from above,
And make our hearts o'erflow with love;
With patience firm and virtue high
The weakness of our flesh supply.

Far from us drive the foe we dread,
And grant us Thy true peace instead;
So shall we not, with Thee for guide,
Turn from the path of life aside.

Oh, may Thy grace on us bestow
The Father and the Son to know,
And Thee through endless times confessed
Of both the eternal Spirit blest.

AVE MARIS STELLA

Hail, bright star of ocean,
God's own Mother blest,
Ever sinless Virgin,
Gate of heavenly rest.

Taking that sweet Ave
Which from Gabriel came,
Peace confirm within us,
Changing Eva's name.

Break the captives' fetters,
Light on blindness pour,
All our ills expelling,
Every bliss implore.

Show thyself a Mother;
May the Word Divine,
Born for us thy Infant,
Hear our prayers through thine.

Virgin all excelling,
Mildest of the mild,
Freed from guilt, preserve us,
Pure and undefiled.

Keep our life all spotless,
Make our way secure,
Till we find in Jesus
Joy forevermore.

Through the highest heaven
To the Almighty Three,
Father, Son and Spirit,
One same glory be. Amen.

MY BREAST PLATE

Christ be with me, Christ within me,
Christ behind me, Christ before me,
Christ beside me, Christ to win me,
Christ to comfort and restore me,
Christ beneath me, Christ above me,
Christ in quiet, Christ in danger,
Christ in hearts of all that love me,
Christ in mouth of friend and stranger

St. Patrick

ASKING

I asked God for strength, that I might achieve...
I was made weak, that I might learn humbly to obey.
I asked for health, that I might do greater things...
I was given infirmity, that I might do better things.
I asked for riches, that I might be happy...
I was given poverty, that I might be wise.
I asked for power, that I might have the praise of men...
I was given weakness, that I might feel the need of God.
I asked for all things, that I might enjoy life...
I was given life, that I might enjoy all things.
I got nothing that I asked for, but everything that
I had hoped for.
Almost despite myself, my unspoken prayers
were answered.
I am among all men, most richly blessed!

Anonymous

148

"My Lady and my Mother, remember I am yours; protect and defend me as your property and possession.

Eucharistic Heart of Jesus, have mercy on us!

O Jesus in the Blessed Sacrament, have mercy on us.

Blessed be the Most Sacred Heart of Jesus in the Holy Eucharist!

O Mary, Mother of God and Mother of mercy, pray for us and for all who have died in the embrace of the Lord.

O Mary, who entered the world without stain; do thou obtain for me from God, that I may leave it without sin,

Glory, love and thanksgiving be to the Sacred Heart of Jesus!"

PRAYER TO ST. FRANCES XAVIER CABRINI

Almighty and Eternal Father, Giver of all Gifts, show us Thy mercy, and grant, we beseech Thee, through the merits of Thy faithful Servant, Saint Frances Xavier Cabrini, that all who invoke her intercession may obtain what they desire according to the good pleasure of Thy Holy Will. (here name your request)

St. Frances Xavier Cabrini, beloved spouse of the Sacred Heart of Jesus, intercede for us that the favor we now ask may be granted.

PRAYER OF ST. FRANCIS OF ASSISI

Lord, make me an instrument of Your peace.
Where there is hatred, let me sow love;
Where there is injury, pardon;
Where there is doubt, faith;
Where there is despair, hope;
Where there is darkness, light;
And where there is sadness, joy.
O Divine Master, grant that I may not so much seek to
be consoled as to console; to be understood as to
understand; to be loved as to love. For it is in giving
that we receive, it is in pardoning that we are pardoned,
and it is in dying that we are born to eternal life.

THERE'S A REASON

For every pain, that we must bear,
    For every burden, every care,
        There's a reason.
For every grief, that bows the head,
    For every tear-drop that is shed,
        There's a reason.
For every hurt, for every plight,
    For every lonely, pain racked night,
        There's a reason.
But if we trust God, as we should,
    It all will work out for our good,
        He knows the reason.

TO EVERYTHING THERE IS A SEASON
AND A TIME TO EVERY PURPOSE
UNDER HEAVEN

A time to be born
   and a time to die
A time to plant
   and a time to reap
A time to laugh
   and a time to weep
A time to embrace
   and a time to not embrace
A time to speak
   and a time to be silent
A time to love
   and a time to hate
A time of war
   and a time of peace

Book of Ecclesiastes

SERENITY PRAYER

GOD grant me the SERENITY to accept the things
I cannot change
COURAGE to change the things I can and
WISDOM to know the difference

THE BLESSING BEFORE MEALS

Bless us O Lord, and these Thy gifts, which we are about to receive from Thy bounty, through Christ Our Lord. Amen

GRACE AFTER MEALS

We give You thanks for all your benefits O' Almighty God, who lives and reigns forever and may the souls of the faithful departed, through the mercy of God, rest in peace. Amen.

ANGEL'S PRAYER AT FATIMA

O MOST HOLY TRINITY FATHER, SON AND HOLY GHOST I ADORE THEE PROFOUNDLY I OFFER THEE THE MOST PRECIOUS BODY, BLOOD, SOUL AND DIVINITY OF JESUS CHRIST PRESENT IN ALL THE TABERNACLES OF THE WORLD, IN REPARATION FOR THE OUTRAGES, SACRILEGES AND INDIFFERENCE BY WHICH HE IS OFFENDED. BY THE INFINITE MERITS OF THE MOST SACRED HEART OF JESUS, AND THE IMMACULATE HEART OF MARY, I BEG THE CONVERSION OF YOU POOR SINNERS.
(Repeat 3 times)

PARDON PRAYER (FATIMA)

My God, I believe, I adore,I trust and I love Thee. I beg pardon for those who do not believe, do not adore, do not trust, and do not love Thee.

≈≈≈≈≈≈≈≈≈≈≈≈≈≈≈≈≈≈≈≈≈≈≈≈≈≈≈≈≈≈≈≈≈≈≈≈≈≈≈

"O my Jesus, I offer this for love of Thee, for the conversion of poor sinners, and in reparation for all the sins committed against the Immaculate Heart of Mary."

EUCHARISTIC OFFERING
FOR OUR HOLY FATHER

Eternal Father, in union with the Immaculate Heart of Mary, I offer Thee the precious Body and Blood, Soul and Divinity of Thy dearly beloved Son, Our Lord, Jesus Christ, truly present in this the Most Blessed Sacrament for the needs and intentions of Our Holy Father, Pope John Paul II.

POPE JOHN PAUL II

THE LITANY OF THE SAINTS

Lord, have mercy.
> *Christ, have mercy.*

Lord, have mercy.

Christ, hear us.
> *Christ, graciously hear us.*

God the Father of heaven, *have mercy on us.*

God the Son, Redeemer of the world,
> *have mercy on us.*

God the Holy Spirit, *have mercy on us.*

Holy Trinity, one God, *have mercy on us.*

Holy Mary, *Pray for us.*

Holy Mother of God, *etc.*

Holy Virgin of virgins,

St Michael,

St. Gabriel,

St. Raphael,

All you holy Angels and Archangels,

All you holy orders of blessed Spirits,

St. John the Baptist,

St. Joseph,

All you holy Patriarchs and Prophets,

St. Peter,

St. Paul,

St. Andrew,

St. James,

St. John,

St. Thomas, *Pray for us.*
St. James, *etc.*
St. Philip,
St. Bartholomew,
St. Matthew,
St. Simon,
St. Thaddeus,
St. Matthias,
St. Barnabas,
St. Luke,
St. Mark,
All you holy Apostles and Evangelists,
All you holy Disciples of our Lord,
All you holy Innocents,
St. Stephen,
St. Lawrence,
St. Vincent,
Sts. Fabian and Sebastian,
Sts. John and Paul,
Sts. Cosmas and Damian,
Sts. Gervase and Protase,
All you holy Martyrs,
St. Sylvester,
St. Gregory,
St. Ambrose,
St. Augustine,
St. Jerome,

St. Martin, *Pray for us.*
St. Nicholas, *etc.*
All you holy Bishops and confessors,
All you holy Doctors,
St. Anthony,
St. Benedict,
St. Bernard,
St. Dominic,
St. St. Francis,
All you holy priests and levites,
All you holy monks and hermits,
St. Mary Magdalen,
St. Agatha,
St. Cecilia,
St. Catherine,
St. Anastasia,
All you holy virgins and widows,
All you holy men and women, Saints of God,
    make intercession for us.
Be merciful, *graciously hear us, O Lord.*
From all evil, *O Lord, deliver us.*
From all sin, *etc.*
From Your wrath.

LITANY OF THE GUARDIAN ANGEL

Try to have a tender love for your Guardian Angel. He never leaves you from the time you come into the world until you leave it in death. Pray to him and always feel that he is close beside you and sees all your actions.

Lord, have mercy on us.
Christ, have mercy on us.
Lord, have mercy on us.
Christ, hear us.
Christ, graciously hear us,
God, the Father of Heaven, *have mercy on us.*
God, the Son, Redeemer of men,
have mercy on us.
God, the Holy Spirit, Sanctifier of souls,
have mercy on us.
Holy Trinity, one God, *have mercy on us.*
Holy Mary, Queen of Heaven, *pray for us.*
Holy Angel, my Guardian, *pray for us.*
Holy Angel, my Protector in all dangers,
Holy Angel, my Defense in all afflictions,
Holy Angel, my most faithful Lover,
Holy Angel, my preceptor,
Holy Angel, my Guide,
Holy Angel, Witness of all my actions,
Holy Angel, my Helper in all my difficulties,
Holy Angel, my Negotiator with God,
Holy Angel, my Advocate,
Holy Angel, lover of Chastity,
Holy Angel, lover of Innocence,

Holy Angel most obedient to God,
Holy Angel, Director of my soul,
Holy Angel, model of Purity,
Holy Angel, model of Docility,
Holy Angel, my Counselor in doubt,
Holy Angel, my Guardian through life,
Holy Angel, my shield at the hour of Death,
    Pray for us
Lamb of God, who takes away the sins of the world, *spare us, O Lord.*
Lamb of God, who takes away the sins of the world, *hear us, O Lord.*
Lamb of God, who takes away the sins of the world, *have mercy on us.*

PRAYER

O God, who with unspeakable providence vouchsafe to send Thy Angels to be our Guardians, mercifully grant, that we, Thy suppliants, may be always defended by their protection and enjoy their eternal society, through Jesus Christ, Thy Son, Our Lord, who lives and reigns with You, in the unity of the Holy Spirit, one God, world without end. Amen. "ANGEL OF GOD, MY GUARDIAN DEAR. TO WHOM HIS LOVE COMMITS ME HERE. EVER THIS DAY BE AT MY SIDE. TO LIGHT, TO GUARD, TO RULE AND GUIDE!" AMEN.

PRAYERS TO THE HOLY SPIRIT

LITANY OF THE HOLY SPIRIT

Lord, have mercy on us.
> *Christ, have mercy on us.*

Lord, have mercy on us. Father all powerful,
> *Have mercy on us.*

Jesus, Eternal Son of the Father, Redeemer of
the world,
> *Save us.*

Spirit of the Father and the Son, boundless
Life of both,
> *Sanctify us.*

Holy Trinity,
> *Hear us.*

Holy Spirit Who proceedest from the Father and the
Son, *enter our hearts.*
Holy Spirit Who art equal to the Father and the
Son, *enter our hearts.*
Promise of God the Father, *have mercy on us.*
Ray of heavenly light, *have mercy on us.*
Author of all good, *etc.*
Source of heavenly water,
Consuming Fire,
Ardent Charity, *have mercy on us.*

Spiritual Unction, *have mercy on us.*
Spirit of love and truth, *etc.*
Spirit of wisdom and understanding,
Spirit of counsel and fortitude,
Spirit of knowledge and piety,
Spirit of the fear of the Lord,
Spirit of grace and prayer,
Spirit of peace and meekness,
Spirit of modesty and innocence,
Holy Spirit the Comforter,
Holy Spirit Who governest the Church,
Gift of God the Most High,
Spirit Who fillest the universe,
Spirit of the adoption of the children of God,

Holy Spirit, *inspire us with the horror of sin.*
Holy Spirit, *come and renew the face of the earth.*
Holy Spirit, *shed Thy light into our souls.*
Holy Spirit, *engrave Thy law in our hearts.*
Holy Spirit, *inflame us with the flame of Thy love.*
Holy Spirit, *open to us the treasures of Thy graces.*
Holy Spirit, *teach us to pray well.*
Holy Spirit, *enlighten us with Thy heavenly
    inspirations.*
Holy Spirit, *Our Greatest Friend.*

Holy Spirit, *lead us in the way of salvation.*
Holy Spirit, *grant us the only necessary knowledge.*
Holy Spirit, *inspire in us the practice of good.*
Holy Spirit, *grant us the merits of all virtues.*
Holy Spirit, *make us persevere in justice.*
Holy Spirit, *be Thou our everlasting reward*

Lamb of God, Who takest away the sins of the world, *Send us Thy Holy Spirit.*
Lamb of God, Who takest away the sins of the world, *Pour down into our souls the gifts of the Holy Spirit.*
Lamb of God, Who takest away the sins of the world, *Grant us the Spirit of Wisdom and piety.*

V. Come, Holy Spirit! Fill the hearts of Thy faithful,
R. *And enkindle in them the fire of Thy love.*

Let Us Pray:

Grant, O merciful Father, that Thy Divine Spirit may enlighten, inflame and purify us, that He may penetrate us with His heavenly dew and make us fruitful in good works, through Our Lord Jesus Christ, Thy Son, who with Thee, in the unity of the same Spirit, liveth and reigneth forever and ever.
R. *Amen.*

162

LITANY FOR THE CHURCH

Lord, *have mercy on us.*
Christ, *have mercy on us.*
Lord, *have mercy on us.*
Christ, Divine Founder of the Church, *hear us.*
Christ, Who warned of false prophets,
    graciously hear us.
God, the Father of heaven, *have mercy on us.*
God, the Son, Redeemer of the World,
    have mercy on us.
God, the Holy Ghost, *have mercy on us.*
Holy Trinity, One God, *have mercy on us.*

Holy Mary, Mother of the Church, *pray for us.*
St. Joseph, Patron of the Universal Church,
    pray for us.
St. Michael, Defender of the Day of Battle,
    pray for us.
St. Peter, the Rock upon which Christ built His
    Church, *pray for us.*
St. Francis of Assisi, Re-Builder of the Church,
    pray for us.
St. Anthony, *pray for us.*
St. Pius V, *pray for us.*
St. Pius X, Foe of Modernism, *pray for us.*

All you Holy Angels and Archangels, *pray that we may resist the snares of the devil.*

St. Catherine of Siena, *pray that Christ's Vicar may oppose the spirit of the world.*

St. John Fisher, *pray that bishops may have the courage to combat heresy and irreverence.*

St. Francis Xavier, *pray that zeal for souls may be re-enkindled in the clergy.*

St. Charles Borromeo, *pray that seminaries may be protected from false teachings.*

St. Vincent de Paul, *pray that seminarians may return to a life of prayer and meditation.*

St. Therese of the Child Jesus, *pray that religious may re-discover their vocation of love and sacrifice.*

St. Thomas More, *pray that the laity may not succumb to the Great Apostasy.*

St. Francis de Sales, *pray that the Catholic Press may again become a vehicle of Truth.*

St. John Bosco, *pray that our children may be protected from immoral and heretical instruction.*

St. Pascal, *pray that profound reverence for the Most Blessed Sacrament may be restored.*

St. Dominic, *pray that we may ever treasure the Holy Rosary.*

Lamb of God, *Who take away the sins of the world, spare us, O Lord;*

Lamb of God, *Who take away the sins of the world,*
graciously hear us, O Lord;
Lamb of God, *Who take away the sins of the world,*
have mercy on us.

Christ, *hear us.*
Christ, *graciously hear us.*

Pray for us, *O Holy Mother of God,*
That we may be made worthy of the promises
of Christ.

LET US PRAY

Jesus our God, in these dark hours when Your
Mystical Body is undergoing its own Crucifixion,
and when it would almost seem to be abandoned by
God the Father, have mercy, we beg of You, on Your
suffering Church. Send down upon us the Divine
Consoler, to enlighten our minds and strengthen
our wills.

You, O Second person of the Most Blessed
Trinity, Who can neither deceive nor be deceived,
have promised to be with Your Church until the end
of time. Give us a mighty faith that we may not
falter; help us to do Your Holy Will always, especially during these hours of grief and uncertainty.
May Your Most Sacred Heart and the Immaculate
and Sorrowful Heart of Your Holy mother, be our
sure refuge in time and in eternity. Amen.

FOOTPRINTS

I dreamed I was walking along the beach with
the Lord...
Across the sky flashed scenes from my life
and for each scene I noticed two sets of footprints.

One set belongs to me—the other to the Lord.
But I also noticed that many times during my life
there was only one set of footprints,
and it always happened at the very lowest and
saddest times in my life.
I couldn't understand this, and so I questioned
the Lord about it:

"Lord, you said you would walk with me all
through my life but I see that during the hardest and
saddest times I've had, there is only one set
of footprints. How could you leave me when I
needed you the most?"

The Lord replied, "My precious child, I love you
and I would never leave you during your times
of grief and suffering. When you saw only one
set of footprints, it was then that I carried you."

Author Unknown

166

LISTEN TO ME

Just stop a while and listen to Me;
I have a question to ask of thee—
Why are you ignoring My Mother?

I chose Her to be My very own, and greater perfection was never known.
Why are you ignoring My Mother?

I was born through Her so we all would be spiritual members of one family.
Why are you ignoring My Mother?

I've sent her to you with a message Divine not once or twice, but many a time.
And still you're ignoring My Mother.

Like a wreath of graces, Her rosary, she's given to Her loving children as a key to heaven.
And still you're ignoring My Mother!

She came with My message to LaSalette, but those requests have not been met.
Why are you ignoring My Mother?

I sent Her again to the cave at Lourdes, but just as before you spurned Her words.
Why are you ignoring My Mother?

167

To the fields of Fatima, again She came for prayers and sacrifice in Her Son's name.
And still you're ignoring My Mother!

She descended again to Medjugorje, but you're not heeding Her latest call.
Why are you ignoring My Mother?

I sent Her to earth from heaven above, so you would give Her your honor and love.
And still you're ignoring My Mother!

When you ignore My Mother, you ignore Her Son because to Me She's the dearest one.
Why are you ignoring My Mother?

You'd better amend and do not tarry. The ideal way to Jesus is Mary!
So stop ignoring My Mother!

Anonymous

Oh Mother Mary, Queen of Peace, we come in the name of all mothers to consecrate our lives to you, and ask you to guide us, as we gather mothers thoughout the world, to pray for peace. Mother, please take all that is in our hearts and present it to your Son, Jesus, the Prince of Peace. Return to us then, all of the graces that only He can give, to unite our wills to His Most Devine Will ... so that we may have peace in our hearts, our homes, our nation and all the nations of the world. Amen

Notes or favorite prayer.

READ THE SCRIPTURES

SCRIPTURE

" I have esteemed the words of His mouth more than my necessary food"

(Job)

" Christ's message in all its richness must live in all your hearts"

(Col. 3:16)

" All scripture is inspired by God and is useful for teaching the truth, rebuking error, correcting faults, and giving instructions for right living, so that the person that serves God may be fully qualified and equipped to do every kind of good deed.

(2 Timothy 3: 16-17)

MATTHEW 6:24-34; 7:1-14

"No one can be a slave of two masters; he will
hate one and love the other; he will be loyal to one
and despise the other. You cannot serve both
God and money.

So my counsel is: Don't worry about "things"—
food, drink, and clothes. For you already have life
and a body-and they are far more important than
what to eat and wear. Look at the birds! They don't
worry about what to eat—they don't need to sow or
reap or store up food—for your heavenly Father
feeds them. And you are far more valuable to Him
than they are. Will all your worries add a single
moment to your life?

And why worry about your clothes? Look at the
field lilies! They don't worry about theirs. Yet King
Solomon in all his glory was not clothes as beautifully as they. And if God cares so wonderfully for
flowers that are here today gone tomorrow, won't
He more surely care for you, O men of little faith?

So don't worry at all about having enough food and
clothing. Why be like the heathen? For they take
pride in all these things and are deeply concerned
about them. But your heavenly Father already
knows perfectly well that you need them, and He

172

will give them to you if you give Him first place in your life and live as He wants you to.

So don't be anxious about tomorrow. God will take care of your tomorrow too. Live one day at a time. Don't criticize, and then you won't be criticized. For others will treat you as you treat them. And why worry about a speck in the eye of a brother when you have a board in your own? Should you say, 'Friend, let me help you get that speck out of your eye', when you can't even see because of the board in your own? Hypocrite! First get rid of the board. Then you can see to help your brother.

Don't give holy things to depraved men. Don't give pearls to swine! They will trample the pearls and turn and attack you.

Ask, and you will be given what you ask for. Seek, and you will find. Knock, and the door will be opened. For everyone who asks, receives. Anyone who seeks, finds. If only you will knock, the door will open. If a child asks his father for a loaf of bread, will he be given a stone instead? If he asks for fish, will he be given a poisonous snake? Of course not! And if you hardhearted, sinful men know how to give good gifts to your children, won't your Father in heaven even more certainly give

good gifts to those who ask Him for them?
Do for others what you want them to do for
you. This is the teaching of the laws of Moses
in a nutshell.

Heaven can be entered only through the narrow
gate! The highway to hell is broad, and its gate is
wide enough for all the multitudes who choose its
easy way. But the Gateway to Life is small, and the
road is narrow, and only a few ever find it.

LOVE IS

Love is patient and kind; it is not jealous or con-
ceited or proud; love is not ill-mannered or selfish
or irritable; love does not keep a record of wrongs;
love is not happy with evil, but is happy with the
truth. Love never gives up; and its faith, hope, and
patience never fail. Love is eternal. There are
inspired messages, but they are temporary; there are
gifts of speaking in strange tongues, but they will
cease; there is knowledge, but it will pass.

1 COR 13:4-8

BOOK OF WISDOM 9:9-11

And with Thee is wisdom, who is familiar with Thy
works and was present at the making of the world
by Thee, who know what is acceptable to Thee in
line with Thy commandments. Send her forth from
Thy holy heavens, and from Thy glorious throne bid
her come down, so that she may labor at my side
and I may learn what pleases Thee. For she knows
and understands all things and will guide me pru-
dently in all I do, and guard me in her glory.

EPHESIANS 3:14-19

For this reason I kneel before the Father, from
whom His whole family in heaven and on earth
derives its name. I pray that out of His glorious
riches He may strengthen you with power through
His Spirit in your inner being, so that Christ may
dwell in your hearts through faith. And I pray that
you, being rooted and established in love, may have
power, together with all the saints, to grasp how
wide and long and high and deep is the love of
Christ, and to know this love that surpassed knowledge—that you may be filled to the measure of all
the fullness of God.

EPHESIANS 6:10-18

Finally, be strong in the Lord and in His mighty power. Put on the full armor of God so that you can take your stand against the devil's schemes. For our struggle is not against flesh and blood, but against the rulers, against the powers and authorities of this dark world and against the spiritual forces of evil in the heavenly realms. Therefore put on the full armour of God, so that when the day of evil comes, you may be able to stand your ground, and after you have done everything, to stand, firm with the belt of truth buckled around your waist, with the breast-plate of righteousness in place, and with your feet fitted with readiness that comes from the gospel of peace. In addition to all this, take up the shield of faith, with which you can extinguish all the flaming arrows of the evil one. Take the helmet of salvation and sword of the Spirit, which is the Word of God. And pray in the Spirit on all occasions with all kinds of prayers and requests. With this in mind, be alert and always keep praying for all the saints.

EPHESIANS 1:11

All things are done according to God's plan and decision; and God chose us to be His own people in union with Christ because of His own purpose, based on what He had decided from the very beginning.

EPHESIANS 1:15-19

For this reason, ever since I heard of your faith in the Lord Jesus and your love for all of God's people, I have not stopped giving thanks to God for you. I remember you in my prayers and ask the God of Our Lord Jesus Christ, the glorious Father to give you the spirit who will make you wise and reveal God to you, so that you will know Him. I ask that your minds be opened to see His light, so that you will know what is the hope to which He has called you, how rich are the wonderful blessings He promises His people, and how very great is His power at work in us who believe.

Notes or favorite prayer.

PRAY THE PSALMS

PSALMS 68:1
God rises up and scatters His enemies.
Those who hate Him run away in defeat.

PSALMS 46:10
"Be still and know that I am God"

PSALMS 23:1-6
The Lord is my shepherd; I have everything I need.
He lets me rest in fields of green grass and leads me
to quiet pools of fresh water.
He gives me new strength. He guides me in the right
paths, as he has promised.
Even if I go through the deepest darkness, I will not
be afraid, Lord, for You are with me. Your
shepherd's rod and staff protect me
You prepare a banquet for me, where all my enemies can see me; You welcome me as an honored
guest and fill my cup to the brim.
I know that your goodness and love will be with me
all my life; and Your house will be my home as
long as I live.

PSALM 91: 1-16

Whoever goes to the Lord for safety, whoever remains under the protection of the Almighty, can say to Him,

"You are my defender and protector. You are my God; in You, I trust."

He will keep you safe from all hidden dangers and from all deadly diseases.

He will cover you with his wings; you will be safe in His care; His faithfulness will protect and defend you.

You need not fear any dangers at night or sudden attacks during the day, or the plagues that strike in the dark or the evils that kill in daylight.

A thousand may fall dead beside you, ten thousand all around you, but you will not be harmed.

You will look and see how the wicked are punished. You have made the Lord your defender, the Most High your protector, and so no disaster will strike you, no violence will come near your home.

God will put his angels in charge of you to protect you wherever you go.

They will hold you up with their hands to keep you from hurting your feet on the stones.

You will trample down lions and snakes, fierce lions and poisonous snakes.

God says, "I will save those who love Me and will

180

protect those who acknowledge Me as Lord.
When they call to Me, I will answer them; when
they are in trouble, I will be with them. I will rescue
them and honor them.
I will reward them with long life; I will save them."

PSALM 100:1-5
Sing to the Lord, all the world!
Worship the Lord with joy;
come before him with happy songs!
Acknowledge that the Lord is God.
He made us, and we belong to Him; we are His
people, we are His flock.
Enter the Temple gates with thanksgiving; go into
its courts with praise. Give thanks to Him and
praise Him.
The Lord is good; His love is eternal and His faith-
fulness lasts forever.

Pieta by Michelangelo at St. Peter's Basilica, Rome.

NOVENAS

FRUITS OF THE HOLY SPIRIT
Gal 5:22

**LOVE, JOY, PEACE, PATIENCE, KINDNESS,
GOODNESS, FAITHFULNESS, HUMILITY,
CHARITY AND SELF-CONTROL.**

GIFTS FO THE HOLY SPIRIT

**WISDOM, UNDERSTANDING, COUNSEL,
FORTITUDE, KNOWLEDGE, PIETY
AND FEAR OF THE LORD**

NOVENA
TO THE
HOLY SPIRIT**

Introduction

No one could possibly love you more than God the Holy Spirit. You have given and received only natural love. God's love is supernatural. His love for you is unlimited.

He created you. Just as you are. Just as He wanted you to be. He wants you to know Him. He wants you to be happy and enjoy this world and this life He gave you.

With His gifts, He gives you all you need to accomplish this. He wants to give you unlimited WISDOM, KNOWLEDGE and UNDERSTANDING. He wants to COUNSEL you and give you FORTITUDE. He wants to make it easy for you to be close and intimate with Him through His gift to you of PIETY. He wants to create in you a love for Him that will satisfy every want and desire you have.

When Jesus lived on the earth with His disciples, they were content to give up everything to follow Him, just to be near Him. With Him, they were safe and if they needed any COUNSEL they knew He could give them the answers. The disciples had never experienced or even heard of such a source of comfort and WISDOM on earth. So when it was time for Him to leave they were very upset. He assured them by telling them He would send the Paraclete, the Comforter to be with them and with all of His followers.

When He lived as a man He could only be touched and seen and known by as many as is humanly possible. By sending His Spirit He could be present, in Spirit, to all, at all times.

The Holy Spirit speaks to you in your thoughts. He prompts or speaks to you in your language, using your grammar and the words you are familiar with and use daily. These thoughts or promptings that come from the Holy Spirit are so natural that unless you are sensitive to His promptings you could easily ignore them or not recognize them as important.

During these nine days reflection on the Holy Spirit, you will pray, meditate, contemplate, ponder, concentrate, reflect, use your imagination and listen.

The author has practiced this devotion from the age of five to the present day (76 years). He has explained this devotion to numerous others who have accepted the information they received from him. Many have been able to apply the devotion to their own lives and are astonished it has not been taught to a greater extent.

Those who have been instructed personally by the author have been able to acquire the devotion in a matter of weeks, months or several years, and even surpassed what he himself has experienced.

Each day, mull over the thought presented to you, for as long as you can. Read and re-read the day. Each time you get a thought, stop and ponder it. Exhaust it before continuing. Your goal is to listen to your thoughts, not to get through it. Imagine there is no such thing as time. Avoid advancing to the following days in an effort to get new information and ideas to fill in the time and blanks you will have. This is precisely what kills meditation. Too much information. Remember, you are not trying to find thoughts and answers from the same sources you are accustomed to using, such as reading. You are trying to hear new thoughts from a different source. This will not be information, this will be KNOWLEDGE. The Holy Spirit will be putting words in your thoughts.

NOTE

At times the author takes the liberty to talk to you as he believes the Holy Spirit has talked to him.

ALSO

The word "You" pertains to your soul when referring to the reader.

186

DAY ONE

HELLO!

O Holy Spirit, I begin this Novena by admitting that I do not KNOW You. I know about You, from what I have been told. I have been told how God the Father, my Creator and God the Son, my Savior, sent You God the Holy Spirit, to be with me. To comfort me, be my advocate, sanctify me.

MUSCLE BUILDER

I am ashamed, after all You have done for me, that I have never taken the time to learn how to open my heart and let You in.

It is my hope, at this moment, You will give me the STRENGTH to be DETERMINED and PERSE-VERE and to constantly have You as my compan-ion. I KNOW how weak I am since I have had other good intentions and failed. I failed in the past because I did not realize it is You who must provide me with Your seven spiritual gifts.

Your gift of FORTITUDE will give me the STRENGTH I need to complete this Novena.

Instill in me, O Holy Spirit, Your gift of FORTI-TUDE so I can carry on, to do what I must do, to complete this Novena

END OF DAY ONE

187

DAY TWO

I'M SORRY

O Holy Spirit, my curiosity has tempted me to begin reading this second day of my Novena instead of spending this time trying to learn how to listen to Your promptings. I always know better than my teacher and did not think it would make any difference. I do not let You guide me because I do not KNOW how to listen to You. In fact, I do not even listen to those who have had the experience of learning how to listen.

WAKE ME UP

Give me Your gift of COUNSEL by reminding me numerous times during this day to talk to You as I would talk to my very best human friend.

COUNSEL me by reminding me to dwell on these thoughts of my first and second day of this Novena.

GIVE ME A SHOVE

Remind me, O Holy Spirit, to express my gratitude to You who have given me so much. My faith, hope and ability to love. My home, friends, relatives and the fact I have life.

Do not let me be one of the nine lepers who did not return to show gratitude.

Thank You, O Holy Spirit, thank You.

END OF DAY TW0

DAY THREE

GET IT!

Already You are giving me, O Holy Spirit, an UNDERSTANDING of how I must spend this moment thinking about You in my heart. You are beginning to let me UNDERSTAND that simply by reading this information will not release Your grace. I am beginning to realize Your gift of UNDER-STANDING comes to me from You, when I take the time to accept Your COUNSEL. For this realization and the gifts You have given me, thank You, O Holy Spirit.

"AND LEAD US NOT INTO_____"

Please do not lead me into temptation, O Holy Spirit! Do not put me to the test that I must prove to You my faith, by making me wait longer to experience Your presence, if for only one second. This second of knowing that You are in my heart will increase my faith. O Holy Spirit, I do believe, help my unbelief.

Make me UNDERSTAND the only reason I am starting this third day of getting to know You is through and with the FORTITUDE You have provided.

If I listen to my pride, I would think I am doing it all by myself.

END OF DAY THREE

189

DAY FOUR

POSSESSED BY THE HOLY SPIRIT

When I look back just these three days, I am beginning to be able to see how my life with You will be much richer as I willingly permit You to take possession of me. This ability to see as You see, to the extent You wish for me to see at this moment, is Your gift of KNOWLEDGE.

Who, O Holy Spirit, in heaven or on earth, possesses the KNOWLEDGE that is Yours and Yours alone?

Why do I spend so much time seeking mere information from others when You are so willing and anxious to give me this gift I need. If only I would take the time to learn how to listen to You.

Why do I put so much importance on money —sex— power— intellectualism—things that do not have a mere fraction of the power You have?

Why do I spend so much time accumulating money when Jesus promised me the Father would provide? What good would it do a man if he gained the whole world and suffered the loss of his soul?

Why do I spend so little time listening to You? Is it my lack of faith? Help me to UNDERSTAND. Show me the way. Lead me, O Kindly Light.

END OF DAY FOUR

190

DAY FIVE

THE CREATOR, THE REDEEMER, THE SANCTIFIER

Have you ever heard of anyone who created, or claimed to have created, a soul, as your Father in heaven has done for you and millions and millions of times over?

Have you ever heard of any creature who has paid the price for a soul in sin, and won salvation for them, as Jesus did for you and millions of others?

I am the Holy Spirit the Third Person of the Trinity. Just as no one other than the Father has the power to create, from nothing, a soul, and just as no one other than the Son has the power to pay the great price for salvation, no one other than I the Holy Spirit has the power to sanctify you.

My child, no one else can explain, teach or give to you My gift of KNOWLEDGE, UNDER-STANDING, COUNSEL, WISDOM, FORTI-TUDE, PIETY AND FEAR OF THE LORD.

I alone can sanctify you and make you worthy to enter Heaven. When you accept these gifts I will reward you with peace, happiness and joy in this life as well as the next.

Give me a chance, have faith in me, ask me your questions.

Many of these questions I have put into your thoughts as a way of leading you. Keep pondering these questions until I give you the answer. Prove to Me your faith. Do not give up, ask for My gift of FORTITUDE— but never give up. Your time has not come to know the answer to some of these questions. I want you to prove your faith to Me.

You want to know how to recognize the Holy Spirit when I talk to you? I am the only one who can answer this question. Never stop listening for My answer.

END OF DAY FIVE

DAY SIX

COME

If you take the time to learn to listen to Me, I will give you My gift of PIETY. This gift will make you want to be near and close to Me. This gift, if you use it, will bring you to ecstasy in My intimacy. This gift will make everything easy for you, but will not interfere with your free will.

I will give you so much. Give Me your appreciation and gratitude.

I AM PEACE

When you learn how to dismiss all distractions and think only of Me in your heart, you will experience Peace. I, your God, My Holy Spirit, is in the midst of this peace you experience. The more undivided attention you focus on Me, the greater and deeper this peace will become.

This peace surrounds Me. I am Peace. You will recognize My presence by this peace.

Do not make the mistake so many others do. Relaxation of the body is not peace.

Peace, My peace that only I can give is of the soul.

Relaxation can be obtained in numerous ways, including— drugs—sex—money. These are of the body and in excess harm the soul.

Your gratitude to Me will increase my gifts to you. Just as you give more to those who appreciate you.

END OF DAY SIX

193

DAY SEVEN

OUT OF ORDER?

Your soul was created to be attracted to Me like steel to a magnet.

If you do not take time to learn to listen to Me, my child, you will become confused, as many others have.

The confused try to satisfy their magnetic attraction to Me by substituting drugs that delight their bodies, and for a short time relaxes them. Some express their confusion by other delights of the body, but this is not the peace I offer you.

The confused not only destroy their bodies and minds, but also their souls.

The confused cannot tell the difference between relaxation of the body and the reward of My peace to their souls.

The confused have refused to listen to Me. All human creatures have been given this right, to refuse to listen. All were created with a will that is free. A free will to choose their Creator or reject Him.

If you learn to listen to Me, I will relieve you of your many anxieties and fears. Your doubts and frustrations will be resolved. You will have Peace.

Your will is free. Choose to make it My will.

END OF DAY SEVEN

DAY EIGHT

LOVE—FEAR

No one, O Holy Spirit, not even You, can cite an occasion that could arise in my life here on earth that cannot be more than satisfied by Your seven gifts.

My love for You, O Holy Spirit, increases as I learn to listen to Your KNOWLEDGE, UNDERSTANDING, and COUNSEL. My love grows as I experience the FORTITUDE and PIETY You give to me.

Increase in me, O Holy Spirit, Your gift of FEAR OF THE LORD so that I will love You so much I cannot offend You out of FEAR of losing You.

Thank You, O Holy Spirit, for Your infinite love.

I know Your great love for me by the mere fact You, the Father and Son, created me and gave me life. Just as I love what I have accomplished, You also love what You have accomplished. IT IS GOOD.

END OF DAY EIGHT

DAY NINE

COMMON SENSE

The only other spiritual gift You offer to us if we listen, O Holy Spirit, is the greatest of all Your gifts. Your gift of WISDOM. This gift of WISDOM is the highest compliment man can receive.

Your gift of WISDOM endows us with the ability to use all of Your other six spiritual gifts in their exact proper proportion.

The baker is wise, O Holy Spirit, when he does not use too much of any one ingredient in his cake. The ability to use each of Your spiritual gifts of KNOWLEDGE—UNDERSTANDING—COUNSEL—FORTITUDE—PIETY and FEAR OF THE LORD in exactly the right proportion is the gift of gifts. The gift of WISDOM.

END OF BEGINNING

This is the ninth day, O Holy Spirit. My intended Novena is completed. I must recognize the fact You gave me the FORTITUDE to persevere. The strength that made it easy. You gave me the determination to succeed as You will in everything You prompt me to do. If only I take time to listen for Your gift of FORTITUDE.

I shall take the time to reminisce on my early childhood and each year up to the present time, to the best of my ability, with Your help and KNOWL-EDGE, O Holy Spirit. I shall dwell on the past few months in particular. You will let me UNDER-STAND how You have been in my life daily, even though I was not aware of it. How You gave me the grace of Your seven gifts and how often I threw them away by neglecting to use them. How on many occasions Your gifts were there and I did use them, but was under the impression, due to my pride, that I did it all by myself.

But, why does it have to end? Why should it end?

If I have not experienced Your presence in my heart, I shall start over for another nine days if You will only give me the FORTITUDE.

If I have experienced Your presence in my heart, I will jealously preserve it. Relive it. Practice listening daily. A perpetual Novena.

My hope is I will grow into the habit of experiencing Your presence every moment of my consciousness.

END OF DAY NINE

CONCLUSION

- **NEVER STOP TRYING.**

- THE HOLY SPIRIT **DEMANDS** FAITH.

- TIME MEANS ABSOLUTELY **NOTHING** TO GOD.

- THIS NOVENA **CANNOT** BE **EXHAUSTED**.

- EVERYTIME YOU MAKE THIS NOVENA, THE **HOLY SPIRIT** WILL **ADD** TO IT.

- WHEN **YOU** PRAY, **YOU** TALK TO GOD.

- WHEN GOD TALKS TO YOU DO **YOU LISTEN**?

**Printed with written permission of the Apostles of the Holy Spirit, Cincinnati, Ohio

NOVENA
TO THE
HOLY SPIRIT

The novena in honor of the Holy Ghost is the oldest of all novenas since it was first made at the direction of Our Lord Himself when He sent His apostles back to Jerusalem to await the coming of the Holy Ghost on the first Pentecost. Addressed to the Third Person of the Blessed Trinity, it is a powerful plea for the light and strength and love so sorely needed by every Christian. To encourage devotion to the Holy Spirit, the Church has enriched this novena with the following indulgences:

"The faithful who devoutly assist at the public novena in honor of the Holy Spirit immediately preceding the Solemn Feast of Pentecost may gain a partial indulgence for themselves or as an offering for the intentions of the faithful departed.

Those who make a private novena in honor of the Holy Spirit, either before the Solemn Feast of Pentecost or at any other time in the year, may also gain a partial indulgence for themselves or as an offering for the intentions of the faithful departed."

ACT OF CONSECRATION TO
THE HOLY SPIRIT

On my knees before the great multitude of heavenly witnesses I offer myself, soul and body to You, Eternal Spirit of God. I adore the brightness of Your purity the unerring keenness of Your justice and the might of Your love. You are the Strength and Light of my soul. In You I live and move and am. I desire never to grieve You by unfaithfulness to grace and I pray with all my heart to be kept from the smallest sin against You. Mercifully guard my every thought and grant that I may always watch for Your light and listen to Your voice and follow Your gracious inspirations. I cling to You and give myself to You and ask You by Your compassion to watch over me in my weakness. Holding the pierced Feet of Jesus and looking at His Five Wounds and trusting in His Precious Blood and adoring His opened Side and stricken Heart I implore You, Adorable Spirit, Helper of my infirmity, so to keep me in Your grace that I may never sin against You. Give me grace, O Holy Spirit, Spirit of the Father and the Son, to say to You always and everywhere "Speak Lord for Your servant heareth." Amen.

(To be recited daily during the Novena)

PRAYER FOR THE SEVEN GIFTS OF THE HOLY SPIRIT

O Lord Jesus Christ Who, before ascending into heaven did promise to send the Holy Spirit to finish Your work in the souls of Your Apostles and Disciples deign to grant the same Holy Spirit to me that He may perfect in my soul the work of Your grace and Your love. Grant me the *Spirit of Wisdom* that I may despise the perishable things of this world and aspire only after the things that are eternal, the *Spirit of Understanding* to enlighten my mind with the light of Your divine truth, the *Spirit of Counsel* that I may ever choose the surest way of pleasing God and gaining heaven, the *Spirit of Fortitude* that I may bear my cross with You and that I may overcome with courage all the obstacles that oppose my salvation, the *Spirit of Knowledge* that I may know God and know myself and grow perfect in the science of the Saints, the *Spirit of Piety* that I may find the service of God sweet and amiable, the *Spirit of Fear* that I may be filled with a loving reverence towards God and may dread in any way to displease Him. Mark me, dear Lord, with the sign of Your true disciples and animate me in all things with Your Spirit. Amen.

(To be recited daily during the Novena)

FIRST DAY
Holy Spirit! Lord of light!
From Your clear celestial height,
Your pure beaming radiance give!

The Holy Spirit
Only one thing is important—eternal salvation. Only one thing, therefore, is to be feared—sin. Sin is the result of ignorance, weakness, and indifference. The Holy Spirit is the Spirit of Light, of Strength, and of Love. With His sevenfold gifts He enlightens the mind, strengthens the will, and inflames the heart with love of God. To ensure our salvation we ought to invoke the Divine Spirit daily, for "The Spirit helpeth our infirmity. We know not what we should pray for as we ought. But the Spirit Himself asketh for us."

PRAYER
Almighty and eternal God, Who hast vouchsafed to regenerate us by water and the Holy Spirit, and hast given us forgiveness of all sins, vouchsafe to send forth from heaven upon us Your sevenfold Spirit, the Spirit of Wisdom and Understanding, the Spirit of Counsel and Fortitude, the Spirit of Knowledge and Piety, and fill us with the Spirit of Holy Fear. Amen.

Our Father and Hail Mary ONCE.
Glory be to the Father SEVEN TIMES.
Act of Consecration, Prayer for the Seven Gifts.

SECOND DAY

Come, Father of the poor!
Come, treasures which endure!
Come, Light of all that live!

THE GIFT OF FEAR

The gift of Fear fills us with a sovereign respect for God, and makes us dread nothing so much as to offend Him by sin. It is a fear that arises, not from the thought of hell, but from sentiments of reverence and filial submission to our heavenly Father. It is the fear that is the beginning of wisdom, detaching us from worldly pleasures that could in any way separate us from God. "They that fear the Lord will prepare their hearts, and in His sight will sanctify their souls."

PRAYER

Come, O blessed Spirit of Holy Fear, penetrate my inmost heart, that I may set You, my Lord and God, before my face forever; help me to shun all things that can offend You, and make me worthy to appear before the pure eyes of Your Divine Majesty in heaven, where You live and reign in the unity of the ever Blessed Trinity, God world without end. Amen

Our Father and Hail Mary ONCE.
Glory be to the Father SEVEN TIMES.
Act of Consecration, Prayer for the Seven Gifts.

THIRD DAY
Thou, of all consolers best,
Visiting the troubled breast,
Dost refreshing peace bestow.

THE GIFT OF PIETY

The gift of Piety begets in our hearts a filial affection for God as our most loving Father. It inspires us to love and respect, for His sake persons and things consecrated to Him, as well as those who are vested with His authority, His Blessed Mother and the Saints, the Church and its visible Head, our parents and superiors, our country and its rulers. He who is filled with the gift of Piety finds the practice of his religion, not a burdensome duty, but a delightful service. Where there is love, there is no labor.

PRAYER

Come, O Blessed Spirit of Piety, possess my heart. Enkindle therein such a love for God, that I may find satisfaction only in His service, and for His sake lovingly submit to all legitimate authority. Amen

Our Father and Hail Mary ONCE.
Glory be to the Father SEVEN TIMES.
Act of Consecration, Prayer for the Seven Gifts.

FOURTH DAY

Thou in toil art comfort sweet;
Pleasant coolness in the heat;
Solace in the midst of woe.

THE GIFT OF FORTITUDE

By the gift of Fortitude the soul is strengthened against natural fear, and supported to the end in the performance of duty. Fortitude imparts to the will an impulse and energy which move it to undertake without hesitancy the most arduous tasks, to face dangers, to trample under foot human respect, and to endure without complaint the slow martyrdom of even lifelong tribulation. "He that shall persevere unto the end, he shall be saved."

PRAYER

Come, O Blessed Spirit of Fortitude, uphold my soul in time of trouble and adversity, sustain my efforts after holiness, strengthen my weakness, give me courage against all the assaults of my enemies, that I may never be overcome and separated from Thee, my God and greatest Good. Amen.

Our Father and Hail Mary ONCE.
Glory be to the Father SEVEN TIMES.
Act of Consecration, Prayer for the Seven Gifts.

FIFTH DAY

Light immortal! Light Divine!
Visit Thou these hearts of Thine,
And our inmost being fill!

THE GIFT OF KNOWLEDGE

The gift of Knowledge enables the soul to evaluate created things at their true worth — in their relation to God. Knowledge unmasks the pretense of creatures, reveals their emptiness, and points out their only true purpose as instruments in the service of God. It shows us the loving care of God even in adversity, and directs us to glorify Him in every circumstance of life. Guided by its light, we put first things first, and prize the friendship of God beyond all else. "Knowledge is a fountain of life to him that possesseth it."

PRAYER

Come, O blessed Spirit of Knowledge, and grant that I may perceive the will of the Father; show me the nothingness of earthly things, that I may realize their vanity and use them only for Thy glory and my own salvation, looking ever beyond them to Thee, and Thy eternal rewards. Amen.

Our Father and Hail Mary ONCE
Glory be to the Father SEVEN TIMES.
Act of Consecration, Prayer for the Seven Gifts.

SIXTH DAY

If Thou take Thy grace away,
Nothing pure in man will stay,
All his good is turn'd to ill.

THE GIFT OF UNDERSTANDING

Understanding, as a gift of the Holy Spirit, helps us to grasp the meaning of the truths of our holy religion. By faith we know them, but by Understanding we learn to appreciate and relish them. It enables us to penetrate the inner meaning of revealed truths and through them to be quickened to newness of life. Our faith ceases to be sterile and inactive, but inspires a mode of life that bears eloquent testimony to the faith that is in us; we begin to "walk worthy of God in all things pleasing, and increasing in the knowledge of God."

PRAYER

Come, O Spirit of Understanding, and enlighten our minds, that we may know and believe all the mysteries of salvation; and may merit at last to see the eternal light in Thy Light; and in the light of glory to have a clear vision of Thee and the Father and the Son. Amen.

Our Father and Hail Mary ONCE.
Glory be to the Father SEVEN TIMES.
Act of Consecration, Prayer for the Seven Gifts.

207

SEVENTH DAY

Heal our wounds — strength renew;
On our dryness pour Thy dew;
Wash the stains of guilt away!

THE GIFT OF COUNSEL

The gift of Counsel endows the soul with supernatural prudence, enabling it to judge promptly and rightly what must be done, especially in difficult circumstances. Counsel applies the principles furnished by Knowledge and Understanding to the innumerable concrete cases that confront us in the course of our daily duty as parents, teachers, public servants, and Christian citizens. Counsel is supernatural common sense, a priceless treasure in the quest of salvation. "Above all these things, pray to the Most High, that He may direct Thy way in truth."

PRAYER

Come, O Spirit of Counsel, help and guide me in all my ways, that I may always do Thy holy will. Incline my heart to that which is good; turn it away from all that is evil, and direct me by the straight path of Thy commandments to that goal of eternal life for which I long. Amen

Our Father and Hail Mary ONCE.
Glory be to the Father SEVEN TIMES.
Act of Consecration, Prayer for the Seven Gifts.

208

EIGHTH DAY

Bend the stubborn heart and will;
Melt the frozen warm the chill;
Guide the steps that go astray!

THE GIFT OF WISDOM

Embodying all the other gifts, as charity embraces all the other virtues. Wisdom is the most perfect of the gifts. Of wisdom it is written "all good things came to me with her and innumerable riches through her hands." It is the gift of Wisdom that strengthens our faith, fortifies hope, perfects charity, and promotes the practice of virtue in the highest degree. Wisdom enlightens the mind to discern and relish things divine, in the appreciation of which earthly joys lose their savor, whilst the Cross of Christ yields a divine sweetness according to the words of the Savior: "Take up Thy cross and follow Me, for My yoke is sweet and My burden light."

PRAYER

Come, O Spirit of Wisdom, and reveal to my soul the mysteries of heavenly things, their exceeding greatness, power and beauty. Teach me to love them above and beyond all the passing joys and satisfactions of earth. Help me to attain them and possess them for ever. Amen.

Our Father and Hail Mary ONCE.
Glory be to the Father SEVEN TIMES.
Act of Consecration, Prayer for the Seven Gifts.

209

NINTH DAY

Thou, on those who evermore
Thee confess and Thee adore,
In Thy sevenfold gifts, descend:
Give them comfort when they die;
Give them life with Thee on high;
Give them joys which never end. Amen

THE FRUITS OF THE HOLY SPIRIT

The gifts of the Holy Spirit perfect the supernatural virtues by enabling us to practice them with greater docility to divine inspiration. As we grow in the knowledge and love of God under the direction of the Holy Spirit, our service becomes more sincere and generous, the practice of virtue more perfect. Such acts of virtue leave the heart filled with joy and consolation and are known as Fruits of the Holy Spirit. These Fruits in turn render the practice of virtue more attractive and become a powerful incentive for still greater efforts in the service of God, to serve Whom is to reign.

PRAYER

Come, O Divine Spirit, fill my heart with Thy heavenly fruits, Thy C*harity, Joy, Peace, Patience*, B*enignity, Goodness, Faith, Mildness*, and T*emperance*, that I may never weary in the service of God, but by continued faithful submission to Thy inspiration may merit to be united eternally with Thee in the love of the Father and Son. Amen.

Our Father and Hail Mary ONCE.
Glory be to the Father SEVEN TIMES.
Act of Consecration, Prayer for the Seven Gifts.

NOVENA PRAYER OF HOLY COMMUNION

Jesus, my Eucharist Friend, accept this Novena of Holy Communions which I am making in order to draw closer to Your dear Heart in sincerest love and to save my soul. If it should be Your Holy Will, grant the special favor for which I am making this Novena. (Mention your request.)

Jesus, You said, "Ask, and it shall be given you; seek and you shall find; knock, and it shall be opened to you" (Matt.7,7). Through the intercession of Your most holy Mother, Our Lady of the Most Blessed Sacrament, I ask, I seek, I knock. I beg of you to grant my request. Grant my prayer!

Jesus, You said, "If you ask the Father anything in My name, He will give it to you" (John 16,23). Through the intercession of Your most holy Mother, Our Lady of the most Blessed Sacrament, I ask the Father in Your name to grant my prayer.

Jesus, You said, "If you ask Me anything in My name, I will do it" (John 14,14). Through the intercession of Your most holy Mother, Our Lady of the most Blessed Sacrament, I ask You in Your name to grant my prayer.

Jesus, You said, "If you abide in Me, and if My words abide in you, ask whatever you will and it shall be done to you" (John 15,7). Through the intercession of Your most holy Mother, Our Lady of the most

Blessed Sacrament, may my request be granted, for I wish to abide in You through frequent Holy Communion. Jesus, I believe in Your love for me!

SEVEN SORROWS

1. The Prophecy of Simeon.
2. The Flight into Egypt.
3. The Loss of the Child Jesus in the Temple.
4. The Meeting of Jesus and Mary on the Way of the Cross.
5. The Crucifixion.
6. The Taking Down of the Body of Jesus from the Cross.
7. The Burial of Jesus.

A POWERFUL NOVENA
TO THE SORROWFUL MOTHER
AND ST. JOSEPH

O Mother of Sorrow, through thy *First Sorrow,* the Prophecy of Holy Simeon, and thine, O St. Joseph, the doubts that harassed thy mind regarding thy chaste Spouse, intercede for me with the Sacred Heart of Jesus, and grant me the favor I implore. (*Here name your request.*)
Our Father, Hail Mary, Glory be.

O Mother of Sorrows, through thy *Second Sorrow,* the Flight into Egypt, and thine,
O St. Joseph, the poverty of the Child Jesus at His

Birth, intercede for me with the Sacred Heart of Jesus, and grant me the favor I implore. (*Here name your request.*)

Our Father, Hail Mary, Glory be.

O Mother of Sorrows, through thy *Third Sorrow,* the Loss of the Child Jesus, and thine, O St. Joseph, intercede for me with the Sacred Heart of Jesus, and grant me the favor I implore. *(Here name your request)*

Our Father, Hail Mary, Glory be.

O Mother of Sorrows, through thy *Fourth Sorrow,* meeting thy Jesus on His Way to Calvary, and thine, O St. Joseph, the Prophecy of Holy Simeon, intercede for me with the Sacred Heart of Jesus, and grant me the favor I implore. *(Here name your request.)*

Our Father, Hail Mary, Glory be.

O Mother of Sorrows, through thy *Fifth Sorrow,* standing beneath Thy dying Son on Mt. Calvary, and thine, O St. Joseph, the Flight into Egypt, intercede for me with the Sacred Heart of Jesus, and grant me the favor I implore. *(Here name your request.)*

Our Father, Hail Mary, Glory be.

O Mother of Sorrows, through thy *Sixth Sorrow,* Thy Jesus is laid in thy Arms, and thine, O St. Joseph, the fear that the tyrant still reigned in Judea, intercede for me with the Sacred Heart of Jesus, and grant me the favor I implore. *(Here name your request)*
Our Father, Hail Mary, Glory be.

O Mother of Sorrows, through thy *Seventh Sorrow,* the Burial of thy Jesus, and thine, O St. Joseph, the three days' Loss of the Child Jesus, intercede for me with the Sacred Heart of Jesus, and grant me the favor I implore. *(Here name your request.)*
Our Father, Hail Mary, Glory be.

Our Lord and Savior, Jesus Christ, we humbly beseech Thee, through Thy Holy Cross and Passion, through Thy Death and glorious Resurrection to be merciful and gracious to us and to all poor sinners.

O Jesus, have mercy on us.

Strengthen our faith; increase our hope; make us perfect in the love of God and our neighbor, so that in this life we may serve Thee alone in true justice, praise and extol Thee forever in Heaven.

NOVENA TO ST. JUDE

Oh, Holy St. JUDE, Apostle & Martyr, great in virtue, rich in miracle, near kinsman of Jesus Christ, Faithful intercessor of all who invoke your special patronage in time of need. To you I have recourse from the depth of my heart and humbly beg to whom God has given such great power to come to my assistance. Help me in my present and urgent petition. In return, I promise to make your name known and cause you to be invoked. Say three Our Fathers, three Hail Marys and Glories for nine consecutive days.

NOVENA TO THE HOLY SPIRIT

Holy Spirit, You, who makes me see everything and shows me the way to reach my ideal. You, who gives me the divine gift to forgive and forget the wrong that is done to me. And You, who are in all the instances of my life with me. I, in this short dialogue, want to thank You for everything and confirm once more that I never want to be separated from you no matter how great the material desires may be. I want to be with You and my loved ones in Your perpetual glory. Amen.

Thank You for Your love towards me and my loved ones. (Persons must pray this 3 consecutive days without asking your request. After the third day your wish will be granted, no matter how difficult it may be. Then promise to publish this dialogue as soon as your favor has been granted.)

NOVENA TO ST. THERESE

ST. THERESE, THE LITTLE FLOWER, PLEASE PICK ME A ROSE FROM THE HEAVENLY GARDEN AND SEND IT TO ME WITH A MESSAGE OF LOVE. ASK GOD TO GRANT ME THE FAVOR, I THEE IMPLORE AND TELL HIM I WILL LOVE HIM EACH DAY MORE AND MORE.

(The above prayer, plus 5 Our Fathers, 5 Hail Marys, 5 Glory Bes, must be said on 5 successive days, before 11 a.m. On the 5th day, the 5th set of prayers having been completed, offer one more set- 5 Our Fathers, 5 Hail Marys, 5 Glory Bes.)

POWERFUL NOVENA
OF CHILDLIKE CONFIDENCE
(This Novena is to be said at the same time every hour for Nine consecutive hours - just one day).

O Jesus, Who hast said, ask and you shall receive, seek and you shall find, knock and it shall be opened to ;you, through the intercession of Mary,

217

Thy Most Holy Mother, I knock, I seek, I ask that my prayer be granted.

(Make your request)
O Jesus, Who hast said, all that you ask of the Father in My Name, He will grant you through the intercession of Mary, Thy Most Holy Mother, I humbly and urgently ask Thy Father in "Thy Name" that my prayer be granted.

(Make your request)
O Jesus, Who hast said, "Heaven and earth shall pass away but My word shall not pass," through the intercession of Mary, Thy Most Holy Mother, I feel confident that my prayer will be granted.
(Make your request)

EFFICACIOUS NOVENA TO THE SACRED HEART OF JESUS

I. O my Jesus, You said, "Verily, I say to you, ask and you shall receive, seek and you shall find, knock and it shall be opened to you," behold I knock, I seek and I ask for the grace of..."

Our Father, Hail Mary, Glory be to the Father.
Sacred Heart of Jesus, I put all my trust in Thee.

218

II. O my Jesus, You said, "Verily, I say to you, whatsoever you shall ask the Father in My name, He will give it to you," behold in your name I ask the Father for the grace of...

Our Father, Hail Mary, Glory be to the Father.
Sacred Heart of Jesus, I put all my trust in Thee.

III. O my Jesus, You said,"Verily, I say to you, heaven and earth shall pass away but My words shall not pass away," behold, I, encouraged by your infallible words, now ask for the grace of...

Our Father, Hail Mary, Glory be to the Father.
Sacred Heart of Jesus, I put all my trust in Thee

O Sacred Heart of Jesus, to whom one thing alone is impossible, namely, not to have compassion on the afflicted, have pity on us miserable sinners and grant us the grace which we ask of Thee through the Sorrowful and Immaculate Heart of Mary, You and Your tender Mother.

Say the Salve Regina and add, St. Joseph, foster father of Jesus, pray for us.

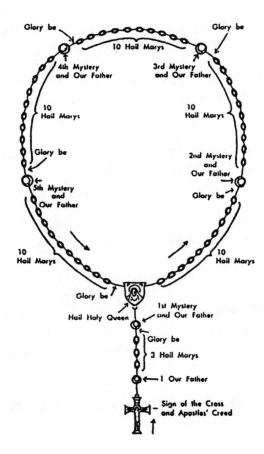

Glory be

Glory be

10 Hail Marys

4th Mystery
and Our Father

3rd Mystery
and Our Father

10
Hail Marys

10
Hail Marys

Glory be

2nd Mystery
and
Our Father

5th Mystery
and
Our Father

Glory be

10
Hail Marys

10
Hail Marys

Glory be

1st Mystery
and Our Father

Hail Holy Queen

Glory be

3 Hail Marys

1 Our Father

Sign of the Cross
and Apostles' Creed

ROSARY

220

THE ROSARY

THE FAMILY THAT PRAYS TOGETHER STAYS TOGETHER

Pray the Rosary! Everytime you pray the rosary say:

*"With this Rosary I bind all my children to the Immaculate Heart of Mary."** *

In doing so, Our Lady promised "to save their souls."

≈≈

*"Come, Holy Spirit, come by means of the powerful intercession of the Immaculate Heart of Mary, Your well-beloved Spouse."** *

≈≈

This Novena consists of reciting five decades of the rosary each day for twenty seven days in petition; then immediately five decades each day for 27 days in thanksgiving, whether or not the request has been granted.

** Printed with permission from the National Headquarters of the Marian Movement of Priests, St. Francis, ME 04774-0008.

THE JOYFUL MYSTERIES
(Said on Mondays, Thursdays, the Sundays of Advent, and Sundays from Epiphany until Lent.)
1. The Annunciation (Humility)
2. The Visitation (Fraternal Charity)
3. The Nativity (Love of God)
4. The Presentation (Spirit of Sacrifice)
5. Finding in the Temple (Zeal)

THE SORROWFUL MYSTERIES
(Said on Tuesdays, Fridays throughout the year; and daily from Ash Wednesday until Easter Sunday.)
1. Agony in the Garden (True Repentance)
2. Scourging at the Pillar (Mortification)
3. Crowning with Thorns (Moral Courage)
4. Carrying of the Cross (Patience)
5. The Crucifixion (Final Perseverance)

THE GLORIOUS MYSTERIES
(Said on Wednesdays, Saturdays, and the Sundays from Easter until Advent.)
1. The Resurrection (Faith)
2. The Ascension (Hope)
3. The Descent of the Holy Spirit (Zeal)
4. The Assumption (Happy Death)
5. The Coronation of B.V.M. (Love for Mary)

"O my Jesus, forgive us our sins, save us from the fires of hell, lead all souls to heaven, especially those in most need of Your mercy.

SIGN OF THE CROSS

In the name of the Father, and of the Son, and of the Holy Spirit. Amen.

THE APOSTLES' CREED

I believe in God, the Father Almighty, Creator of heaven and earth; and in Jesus Christ, His only Son, Our Lord; who was conceived by the Holy Spirit, born of the Virgin Mary, suffered under Pontius Pilate, was crucified, died and was buried. He descended into hell; the third day He arose again from the dead; He ascended into heaven, and sits at the right hand of God, the Father Almighty, from thence He shall come to judge the living and the dead. I believe in the Holy Spirit, the Holy Catholic Church, the communion of saints, the forgiveness of sins, the resurrection of the body, and life everlasting. Amen.

THE OUR FATHER

Our Father who art in heaven, hallowed be Thy name; Thy kingdom come; Thy will be done on earth as it is in heaven. Give us this day our daily bread; and forgive us our trespasses as we forgive those who trespass against us; and lead us not into temptation, but deliver us from evil. Amen.

THE HAIL MARY

Hail Mary, full of grace! the Lord is with thee; blessed are thou among women, and blessed is the fruit of Thy womb, Jesus. Holy Mary, Mother of God, pray for us sinners now and at the hour of our death. Amen.

GLORY BE TO THE FATHER

Glory be to the Father and to the Son, and to the Holy Spirit. As it was in the beginning, is now, and ever shall be, world without end. Amen.

THE HAIL! HOLY QUEEN

Hail! Holy Queen, Mother of Mercy, our life, our sweetness and our hope. To you do we cry, poor banished children of Eve. To you do we send up our sighs, mourning and weeping in this valley of tears. Turn then, O most gracious advocate, your eyes of mercy toward us; and after this our exile, show unto us the blessed fruit of your womb, Jesus. O Clement! O loving! O sweet Virgin Mary!
V. Pray for us, O Holy Mother of God.
R. That we may be made worthy of the promises of Christ.

PRAYER AFTER THE ROSARY

O God, whose only-begotten Son, by His life, death and resurrection, has purchased for us the rewards of eternal life; grant, we beseech Thee, that, meditating upon these mysteries of the Most Holy Rosary of the Blessed Virgin Mary, we may imitate what they contain and obtain what they promise, through the same Christ our Lord. Amen.

PRAYER TO SAINT MICHAEL

Saint Michael, the Archangel, defend us in the day of battle; be our safeguard against the snares of the devil. May God rebuke him, we humbly pray; and do thou, O Prince of the heavenly host, by the divine power of God, cast into hell satan and all other evil spirits who roam throughout the world seeking the ruin of souls. Amen.

PRAYER OF CONSECRATION TO THE SACRED HEART OF JESUS**

Jesus, we know that You are merciful and that You have offered Your heart for us. It is crowned with thorns and with our sins. We know that You implore us constantly so that we do not go astray. Jesus, remember us when we are in sin. By means of Your heart, make all men love one another. Make hate disappear from amongst men. Show us Your love. We all love You and want You to protect us with Your shepherd's heart and free us from every sin. Jesus, enter into every heart! Knock, Knock at the door of our heart. Be patient and never desist. We are still closed because we have not understood Your love. Knock continuously. O good Jesus, make us open our hearts to You, at least in the moment we remember Your passion suffered for us. Amen.

**Dictated by Our Lady to Jelena Vasilj, 11-28-83

CONSECRATION TO THE IMMACULATE HEART OF MARY**

O Immaculate Heart of Mary, ardent with goodness, show your love towards us. May the flame of your Heart, O Mary, descend on all mankind. We love you so. Impress true love in our hearts so that we have a continuous desire for you. O Mary, humble and meek of heart, remember us when we are in sin. You know that all men sin. Give us, by means of your Immaculate Heart, spiritual health. Let us always see the goodness of your maternal heart and may we be converted by the means of the flame of your Heart. Amen.

DAILY RENEWAL OF THE CONSECRATION OF THE FAMILY TO THE MOST SACRED HEART OF JESUS.

Most sweet Jesus, humbly kneeling at Your feet, we renew the consecration of our family to Your Divine Heart. Be our King forever. In You we have full and entire confidence. May Your spirit penetrate our thoughts, our desires, our words and our works. Bless our undertakings, share in our joys, in our trails, and in our labors. Grant us to know You better, to love You more and to serve You without faltering.

By the Immaculate Heart of Mary, Queen of Peace, set up Your kingdom in our country. Enter closely into the midst of our families and make them Your own by the solemn enthronement of Your Sacred Heart so that soon one cry may resound from home to home: May the Sacred Heart of Jesus and the Immaculate Heart of Mary be loved, blessed and glorified forever. Honor and glory be the Sacred Hearts of Jesus and Mary. Sacred Heart of Jesus, protect our families. Amen.

MARY'S ROSARY PROMISES TO ST. DOMINIC

Whosoever shall faithfully pray My Rosary:

1. Shall receive signal graces.
2. Shall have my special protection and the greatest graces.
3. Shall have a powerful armor against hell. It will destroy vice, decrease sin, defeat heresies.
4. Shall find that it will cause virtue and good works to flourish, it will obtain for souls the abundant mercy of God, it will withdraw the hearts of men from the love of the world and its vanities, and will lift them to the desire of eternal things. Oh, that souls would sanctify themselves by this means!

5. Shall not perish.
6. Shall never be conquered by misfortune if he applies himself to the consideration of its sacred mysteries. God will not chastise him in His justice, he will not perish by an unprovided death; if he be just, he shall remain in the grace of God and become worthy of eternal Life.
7. Shall not die without the Sacraments of the Church.
8. Shall have during their life and at their death the Light of God and the plenitude of His graces. At the moment of death they shall participate in the merits of the saints in paradise.
9. Shall be delivered from purgatory.
10. Shall merit a high degree of glory in Heaven.
11. Shall obtain all asked of Me.
12. ...and propagate it, shall be aided by me in their necessities.
13. Shall have for intercessors the entire celestial court during their life and at the hour of death.
14. Are my sons and brothers of my only Son, Jesus Christ.
15. Can consider it a great sign of predestination.

THE GREAT PROMISE OF THE SACRED HEART OF JESUS

"I promise thee in the excessive mercy of My Heart that My all-powerful love will grant to all those who communicate on the First Friday in nine consecutive months, the grace of final penitence; they shall not die in My disgrace nor without receiving their Sacraments. My Divine Heart shall be their safe refuge in this last moment."

THE TWELVE PROMISES OF THE SACRED HEART TO ST. MARGARET MARY

1. I will give them all the graces necessary for their state of life.
2. I will give peace in their families.
3. I will console them in all their troubles.
4. They shall find in My Heart an assured refuge during life and especially at the hour of death.
5. I will pour abundant blessings on all their undertakings.
6. Sinners shall find in My Heart the source and infinite ocean of mercy.
7. Tepid souls shall become fervent.
8. Fervent souls shall speedily rise to great perfection.

9. I will bless the homes in which the image of My Sacred Heart shall be exposed and honored.
10. I will give to priests the power to touch the most hardened hearts.
11. Those who propagate this devotion shall have their name written in My Heart, and it shall never be effaced.
12. The all-powerful love of My Heart will grant to all those who shall receive Communion on the First Friday of nine consecutive months the grace of final repentance; they shall not die under My displeasure, nor without receiving their Sacraments; My Heart shall be their assured refuge at that last hour.

OFFERING OF THE FIRST FRIDAY

O Sacred Heart of Jesus, burning with love for me and most anxious for my love, I wish to spend this entire day in a spirit of love and reparation. I wish my every thought and action to be in praise of Thy love, shown for me in the Blessed Sacrament. Whatever work I do, whatever I may have to suffer, I wish to offer it to Thee through the Immaculate Heart of Mary, that through her I may become more pleasing to Thee. I will try by every means at my disposal to bring others to the knowledge of Thy love. Amen.

Jesus, meek and humble of Heart, make our hearts like unto Thine.
(500 days Indulgence each time)

Sacred Heart of Jesus, Thy Kingdom Come!
(300 days Indulgence each time)

Immaculate Heart of Mary, pray for us now and at the hour of our death.

"Those who promote this devotion shall have their names written in My Heart never to be blotted out." Words of our Blessed Lord.

REQUIREMENTS FOR FIRST FRIDAYS

"The all powerful love of my Heart will grant to those who shall receive Communion on the First Friday of nine consecutive months the grace of final repentance..."

Those who honor Our Lord in his Sacred Heart by attending Mass and receiving Communion for nine consecutive First Fridays would receive many graces from the Heart of Jesus and would not die without receiving the Sacraments.

A final promise was that the Sacred Heart would be an "assured refuge at the last hour." A similar promise was made by Our Lady for those who faithfully practice the First Saturday Devotion.

232

REQUIREMENTS FOR FIRST SATURDAYS

Our Lady promised to assist at the hour of death
with all the graces necessary for salvation for all
those who on the First Saturday of five consecutive
months, confess, receive Holy Communion, recite
five dacades of the Rosary, and keep her company
for fifteen minutes meditating on the mysteries
of the Rosary, with the intention of making
reparation to her.

THE SATURDAY PRAYER

O God, of infinite goodness and mercy, fill our
hearts with a great confidence in our Most Holy
Mother, whom we invoke under the title of the
Immaculate Heart of Mary, and grant us by her most
powerful intercession all the graces, spiritual and
temporal, which we need. Through Christ Our Lord.
Amen.

WHY FIVE SATURDAYS?

Reparation for five kinds of offenses:
1. Blasphemies against the Immaculate
    Conception.
2. Blasphemies against her perpetual virginity.

233

3. Blasphemies against the divine spiritual maternity of Mary.
4. Blasphemies involving the rejection and dishonoring of her images.
5. The neglect of implanting in the hearts of children a knowledge and love of this Immaculate Mother.

Our Lady of Mt. Carmel

235

SACRAMENTALS

HOLY WATER A MEANS OF SPIRITUAL WEALTH

Holy water is a sacramental that remits venial sin. Because of the blessing attached to it, Holy Church strongly urges its use upon her children, especially when dangers threaten, such as fire, storms, sickness and other calamities. Every Catholic home always should have in it a supply of holy water.

We do not take advantage of the benefits derived from holy water.

LET US CULTIVATE ITS USE

Untold spiritual wealth is concentrated in a tiny drop of blessed water.

And we give it so little thought!

Did we realize now, as we shall realize after death, the many benefits which may be derived from holy water, we would use it far more frequently, and with greater faith and reverence.

Holy water has its great power and efficacy from the prayers of the Church, which its Divine Founder always accepts with complacency.

Following are some of the petitions the priest makes to God when he blesses water.

"O God,... grant that this creature of Thine (water) may be endowed with divine grace to drive away devils and to cast out diseases, that whatever in the houses or possessions of the faithful may be sprinkled by this water, may be freed from everything unclean, and delivered from what is hurtful...Let everything that threatens the safety or peace of the dwellers therein be banished by the sprinkling of this water; so that the health which they seek by calling upon Thy Holy Name may be guarded from all assault."

PRAYERS EFFECTIVE

These prayers ascend to heaven each time you take holy water and sprinkle a drop either for yourself or for another, whether he be present or absent; and God's blessings descend for soul and body.

DISPEL THE DEVIL

The devil hates holy water because of its power over him. He cannot long abide in a place or near a person that is often sprinkled with this blessed water.

DO YOUR DEAR ONES
LIVE AT A DISTANCE?

Holy water, sprinkled with faith and piety, can move the Sacred Heart to bless your loved ones and protect them from all harm of soul and body. When worry and fear take possession of your heart, hasten to your holy water font, and give your dear ones the benefit of the Church's prayers.

THE HOLY SOULS LONG FOR IT

Only in Purgatory can one understand how ardently a poor soul longs for holy water. If we desire to make a host of intercessors for ourselves, let us try to realize now some of their yearnings, and never forget them at the holy water font. The holy souls nearest to Heaven may need the sprinkling of only one drop to relieve their pining souls.

REMITS VENIAL SINS

Because holy water is one of the Church's sacramentals, it remits venial sin. Keep your soul beautifully pure in God's sight by making the Sign of the Cross carefully while saying,

"By this holy water and by Thy Precious Blood wash away all my sins, O Lord."

YOUR SCAPULAR

"Whosoever Dies Clothed In This (Scapular) Shall Not Suffer Eternal Fire."

"Wear it devoutly and perseveringly," Our Lady says to each soul, "it is my garment. To be clothed in it means you are continually thinking of me, and I in turn am always thinking of you and helping you to secure eternal life."

St. Alphonsus says:

"Just as men take pride in having others wear their livery, so the most holy Mary is pleased when her servants wear her scapulars as a mark that they have dedicated themselves to her service, and are members of the Family of the Mother of God."

SONGS

The Mission
Immaculate Mary
Holy God, We Praise Thy Name
Dear Lady of Fatima
Bring Flowers of the Rarest
Father I Adore You
Spirit of the Living God
As I Kneel Before You
Hail Queen of Heaven
Salve Regina

≈≈≈≈≈≈≈≈≈≈≈≈≈≈≈≈≈≈≈≈≈≈≈≈≈≈≈≈≈≈≈≈≈≈≈≈

Words to the following songs are found in the Glory and Praise (GP), Music Issue (MI) and Daily Missal (DM)

Be Not Afraid	GP
Prayer to St. Francis	MI
Hail Mary, Gentle Woman	GP
Amazing Grace	GP
Holy God, We Praise Thy Name	DM
Peace is Flowing	GP
Battle Hymn of Republic	MI
Hail, Holy Queen	DM
On This Day O Beautiful Mother	MI
They'll know We are Christians by Our Love	MI
Here I am the Lord	MI
Glory & Praise	MI
Morning has Broken	MI
On Eagle's Wings	MI

240

The Mission

There's a call going out across the land in every nation, a call to all who swear allegiance to the Cross of Christ; a call to true humility, to live our lives responsibly, to deepen our devotion to the Cross at any price.

Let us then be sober, moving only in the spirit, As aliens and strangers in a hostile foreign land. The message we're proclaiming is repentance and forgiveness. The offer of salvation to the dying race of man.

Chorus
To love the Lord our God is the heartbeat of our mission, the spring from which our service over-flows. Across the street or around the world, the mission's still the same, proclaim and live the truth in Jesus' name!

As a candle is consumed by the passion of the flame, spilling light unsparingly throughout a darkened room, let us burn to know him deeper, then our service flaming bright, will radiate His Passions and blaze with holy light.

Repeat Chorus

IMMACULATE MARY

Immaculate Mary your praises we sing.
You reign now in heaven with Jesus our King.

Refrain: Ave, Ave, Ave, Maria! Ave, Ave, Maria!

In heaven the blessed your glory proclaim;
On earth we your children invoke your fair name.

We pray for our Mother, the Church upon earth,
And bless, Holy Mary, the land of our birth.

HOLY GOD, WE PRAISE THY NAME

Holy God, we praise Thy name;
Lord of all, we bow before Thee;
All on earth Thy scepter claim,
All in heaven above adore Thee.
(Refrain - Repeat)
       Infinite Thy vast domain,
       Everlasting is Thy reign!

Hark, the loud celestial hymn;
Angel choirs above are raising;
Cherubim and Seraphim,
In unceasing chorus praising,
(Refrain - Repeat)
       Fill the heavens with sweet accord:
       Holy, holy, holy, Lord!

242

HAIL, HOLY QUEEN

Hail, holy Queen enthroned above, O Maria!
Hail, mother of mercy and of love, O Maria!

Refrain: Triumph, all ye cherubim,
Sing with us, ye seraphim!
Heav'n and earth resound the hymn:
Salve, Salve, Salve Regina!

DEAR LADY OF FATIMA

Ave Maria, Ave Maria, The heavens were opened
Our Lady appeared at Fatima one day
To tell us again of the great need for prayer
As her children, we answer this way
Dear Lady of Fatima
We come on bended knee
To beg your intercession
for peace and unity.
Dear Mary, won't you show us
the right and shining way.
We pledge our love and offer you,
A Rosary each day.

You promised at Fatima,
Each time you appeared,

To help us if we pray to you
To banish war and fear.
Dear Lady on First Saturdays,
We ask your guiding hand
for grace and guidance here on earth,
And protection for our land.

BRING FLOWERS OF THE RAREST

Bring flow'rs of the fairest, bring flowers of the
rarest,
From garden and woodland and hillside and vale;
Our full hearts are swelling, our glad voices
    telling
The praise of the loveliest Rose of the vale.

Refrain:
O Mary! we crown thee with blossoms today,
Queen of the Angels, Queen of the May.
O Mary! we crown thee with blossoms today,
Queen of the Angels, Queen of the May.

Our voices ascending, in harmony blending,
Oh! thus may our hearts turn dear Mother, to
    thee;
Oh! thus shall we prove thee how truly we love thee,
How dark without Mary life's journey would be.

O Virgin most tender, our homage we render,
Thy love and protection, sweet Mother, to win;
In danger defend us, in sorrow befriend us,
And shield our hearts from contagion and sin.
Of mothers the dearest, oh, wilt thou be nearest,
When life with temptation is darkly replete?
Forsake us, O never! our hearts be they ever
As pure as the lilies we lay at thy feet.

FATHER I ADORE YOU

Father I adore You.
Lay my life before You.

Refrain: How I love You.

Jesus I adore You.
Lay my life before You.

Refrain: How I love You.

Spirit I adore You.
Lay my life before You.

Refrain: How I love You.

SPIRIT OF THE LIVING GOD

Spirit of the living God fall afresh on us.
Spirit of the living God fall afresh on us.
Melt us.
Mold us.
Fill us.
Use us.
Spirit of the living God fall afresh on us.

AS I KNEEL BEFORE YOU

Chorus:
Ave Maria, Gratia Plena
Dominus Tecum, Benedicta Tu.
≈≈
As I kneel before you, as I bow my head in
prayer, take this day, make it Yours and fill me
with Your love.
Repeat Chorus:

All I have I give You, every dream and wish are
Yours. Mother of Christ, Mother of mine, present
them to my Lord.
Repeat Chorus:

As I kneel before, You, and I see Your smiling face,
every thought, every word is lost in Your embrace.

HAIL, QUEEN OF HEAVEN

1. Hail, Queen of Heaven, the Ocean Star,
   Guide of the wanderer here below,
   Thrown on life's surge, we claim thy care;
   Save us from peril and from woe.
   Mother of Christ, Star of the Sea,
   Pray for the wanderer, pray for me.

2. O gentle, chaste, and spotless Maid,
   We sinners make our prayers through
   thee; Remind thy Son that He has paid
   The price of our iniquity.
   Virgin most pure, Star of the Sea,
   Pray for the sinner, pray for me.

SALVE REGINA

Salve Regina, Mater misericordiae! Vita, dulcedo, et
spec nostra, salve Ad te calmamus, exules filii Evae.
Ad te suspiramus, gementes, et flentes, in hac
lacrimarum valle. Eia ergo, advocata nostra, illos
tuos misericodes oculos ad nos converte. Et Jesum,
benedictum fructum ventris tui, nobis post hoc
exilium ostende. O clemens, O Pia, O dulcis Virgo
Maria!

JESUS

And thou shalt
call His name Jesus,
Prince of Peace, Mighty God,
Wonderful Counselor, Holy One,
Lamb of God, Prince of Life,
Lord God Almighty,
Lion of the Tribe of Judah,
Root of David, Word of Life,
Author and Finisher of Our Faith,
Advocate, The Way, Dayspring,
Lord of All, I Am, Son of God,
Shepherd and Bishop of Souls,
Messiah, The Truth, Saviour,
Chief Cornerstone, King of Kings,
Righteous Judge, Light of the World,
Head of the Church, Morning Star,
Sun of Righteousness, Lord
Jesus Christ, Chief Shepherd,
Resurrection and Life,
Horn of Salvation, Governor,
The Alpha and Omega.

*SACRED HEART OF JESUS AND THE
IMMACULATE HEART OF MARY*

*The perfect path to Jesus is through Mary.
Mary always leads us to Jesus (we love Jesus
with the heart of Mary.)*

OUR LADY OF
THE NEW ADVENT

Woman of the New Advent, Mother of God,
God-bearer, bearer of light, of truth,
of life and of wisdom...
Humanity stands at a threshold,
a threshold of hope and love;
the threshold of a new millennium
in which your people, the people of your
God, may walk as the Church in unity,
in love, in peace, and in deepest respect
for one another and for all life.
May our dreams of peace be realized,
May our prayers for the coming
of the Kingdom of your Son and God
be answered in our hearts
and in the world God's love has created.

Amen

The image of "Our Lady of the New Advent,"
comes about with the understanding that the 1990's
is the decade of the New Advent, the preparation for
the celebration of the 2000th anniversary of the
Incarnation of Christ our Savior.

Mary wears purple, the color of Advent. Purple symbolizes the dignity of royalty. The Christ child is dressed in a robe of reddish tint. Red symbolizes the priestly class of the chosen People of God.

Mary's arms are raised in the great gesture of love for the world. On one hand she is showing Christ to the world and on the other she is interceding for the world with Christ. Mary wears two golden cuffs on her sleeves which represent the two inseparable natures — the divine and the human.

Mary is crowned with three stars — one on her forehead and one on each breast. The stars represent the crowning virtues of Mary's life. Therefore Mary's life is one of purity, chastity and innocence. They all represent Mary's faith, hope and love. Laity's life should also be crowned with the stars of purity, chastity and innocence, and with the virtues of faith, hope and love.

The Christ child holds a columbine, a symbol of the Holy Spirit and Colorado's state flower. The petals of a single columbine flower form the shape of five doves around the stamen. The single stem of the columbine held by Christ symbolizes the one God. The three blossoms on the stem represent the three persons of the Holy Trinity.

Our Lady of New Advent